Dedication

In memory of President Theodore (Teddy) Roosevelt for his invaluable contribution to the creation of our beloved teddy bear.

Acknowledgments

One of the greatest rewards of being involved with the teddy bear world is the wonderful people I have met. Their willingness to share and their kind cooperation has made my book project very gratifying.

I wish to acknowledge a special debt of gratitude to my friend Georgi Bohrod Rothe for her continued encouragement, assistance and professional guidance. To my photographer Larry McDaniel for his patience and suggestions in photographing endless "groups" of bears. A big thank you to Patricia Matthews and Sara Jinnett for their excellent computer service. My husband Wally's understanding and encouragement throughout these past ten years of authoring seven books, has surpassed all the qualifications for a number one husband. To my editor, Mary Beth Ruddell, my thanks for her invaluable help and cooperation, and my sincere thanks to my publisher, Gary R. Ruddell, for believing in this book.

My gratitude to the following companies and organizations for their assistance.
Applause Inc.; Associated Business Services; Bearly People; Bears in the Attic; Cambridge Consulting Corporation; Carlsbad Village Camera; Charleen Kinser Designs; Cherished Teddies; Commonwealth Toy and Novelty Co., Inc.; Cooperstown Bears; Enesco; Fielding Antiques; Gerald Freeman Inc.; Good Bears of the World; Gund; Hotchkin Bear Company; Knickerbocker Bear Company; Lucy and Me; Mary Meyer Stuffed Toys; North American Bear Co., Inc.; Oz International; *Playthings* magazine; R. Dakin and Company; R. John Wright; Sarah's Attic; Schmid; Smithsonian Institute, Washington, D.C.; The Boyds Collection; The Library of Congress, Washington, D.C.; The U.S. Senate Collection for Legislative Archives, Washington, D.C.; The Vermont Teddy Bear Company; U.S.D.A. Forest Service, Smokey Bear Program, Washington, D.C.

Thank you to the following collectors for sharing their knowledge and their priceless collections with me.
Dottie Ayers; Barbara Baldwin; Rosemarie Binsteiner; Bill Boyd; Susie Carlson; Sydney R. Charles; Sue Coe; Nelson Davis; Flore Emory; Sue and Randall Foskey; Richard Friz; Dot Gillett; April Whitcomb Gustafson; Jim and Martha Hession; Mimi Hiscox; Patricia Johnson; Thelma Kimble; Barbara Lauver; Marilyn and Lee Lewis; Audrey A. Meeneghen; Terry and Doris Michaud; Charles Moose; Susan Nicholson; Robert Raikes; Patricia Schoonmaker; Sherryl Shirran; Helen Sieverling; Karen Silverstein; Pat Todd; Captain Jim Van Meter; Judy Vinson; Robert Welch; Wisconsin River Collection; Joan Woessner; Mort and Evelyn Wood; David Worland; Captain Richard C. Yokley.

If I have omitted someone, please forgive me.

Front Cover: A fine representation of American manufactured bears from the past and present. *Photograph by Larry McDaniel.*
Title Page: Photograph of Theodore Roosevelt. Bear. Unidentified American Manufacturer. Circa 1907; 13in (33cm). *See page 9 for further information.*

Back Cover: (Left) Ideal Bear. Circa 1907. 22in (56cm) short silvery gray mohair; shoe-button eyes; jointed arms and legs; swivel head; excelsior stuffing. (Right) Unidentified American Manufacturer. Bear. Circa 1907. 14in (36cm); short golden colored mohair; shoe-button eyes; jointed arms and legs; swivel head; excelsior stuffing. (Front) Simon & Halbig "Uncle Sam" Portrait Doll. Circa 1900. 14in (36cm); bisque head; glass eyes; composition jointed body. *Photograph by Larry McDaniel.*

Additional copies of this book may be purchased at $29.95 (plus postage and handling) from
HOBBY HOUSE PRESS, INC.
One Corporate Drive
Grantsville, Maryland 21536
or from your favorite bookstore or dealer.

©1995 Linda Mullins

ISBN: 0-87588-432-6

Table of Contents

Chapter One
The American Teddy Bear Scene

No other image represents one of the last symbolic vestiges of human caring and loving in this fast-paced, technological 20th Century than the teddy bear. Now that we can go to the moon, cure rare diseases and run entire business enterprises without ever meeting in person, the teddy bear is a cuddly reminder of a nostalgic past.

Teddy bears go everywhere and do everything. There is not a corner of the globe that they have not penetrated. Their appeal is universal to all countries and to all ages. Sometimes I see teddy bears as missionaries — bringing people throughout the world closer together.

They have gone into battle on guns, tanks and haversacks — saving lives by intercepting bullets. They link home and happiness. They have flown all over the world in airplanes, been drowned in floods, burned in concentration camps, worshipped as totems and used in advertising campaigns. People in all walks of life love teddy bears. Indeed, it makes no difference whether you are rich or poor, distinguished or just an "average Joe," teddy can have precisely the same affect on you. Teddies are collected by movie stars, ballerinas and actresses; used as mascots and talisman. Teddy bears have had endless books, songs and verses written about them. They comfort the sick and bring joy to the young. They are admired as works of art and historic treasures.

Probably no other creature or creation in history has done so much by doing so little. Teddy has never spoken a word, but his presence alone has dispelled fears and given encouragement.

The increase in teddy bear shows, clubs, and shops is a clear manifestation of the continuing growing interest and popularity of teddy bears.

Throughout America, there is a proliferation of teddy bear clubs which are locally and regionally active. One well-respected club, with which I am associated in Southern California, is open to anyone who loves teddy bears, loves to collect teddy bears and arctophiles of any degree. The International League of Teddy Bear Collectors (I.L.T.B.C.) was founded in 1984 (page 6, bottom left.) Its newsletter, *Teddy Bear Tabloid* is a format to share ideas, inform readers of shows, sale offers, as well as advertising for trading, swapping and selling collectible bears. Each summer the club holds an annual convention in Orange, California. They also serve as a donation vehicle for distribution of teddy bears to abused and needy children and adults.

Above: Owning an early teddy bear is even more meaningful when you learn of his provenance or obtain a photograph of the bear with his original owner. Such was my good fortune with the appealing bear in this illustration. The bear belonged to Fred Campell Walker who was born March, 1906 in Tennessee. The bear had been his constant companion since this photograph of Fred taken his second birthday. After her husband had passed away at the age of 80, Fred's wife Beatrice wrote to me about purchasing the bear. Beatrice expressed how much the bear had meant to her husband, and being a boy she was amazed at the care he had taken of it all these years. Her concern was that the bear would continue to be taken good care of after she passed on.

Left: This original pastel by Gisele Nash depicts the security and love a child receives from a teddy bear.

Right: There are many different opinions on determining material value of a bear. Bears with a certain provenance, family heirlooms, childhood treasures, bears whose fur and/or condition portray generations of love (such as these much-loved early 1900s American bears) have more value to their owner than any bear imaginable. *Courtesy Audrey Vasta.*

Below left: The Wood home is an enchanted cottage, filled with childhood innocence, wonderment and fantasy. The Wood collection includes large and small teddy bears, stuffed animals of all kinds and wood carvings and ceramics. The Wood's home serves as a special retreat for Evelyn who is an administrator for urban jails and Mort, a full-time dentist. *Courtesy Mort and Evelyn Wood.*

Below right: Jim and Martha Hession's love of early American Bears grew out of their lifelong interest in American History. Martha says: "The infinite variety and uniqueness of early American bears appealed to us, and they were generally more affordable. Helen Sieverling convinced me to restore my own bears, and I listened and read everything I could; always remembering that 'Teddy is a Textile' has helped me immensely. After working on 50 or more bears, I have decided that I am really a preservationist rather than a restorer. I preserve all I can of the original bear. A bear that stays dirty will eventually weaken and disintegrate and you will lose a friend and an investment!" *Courtesy Jim and Martha Hession.*

5

Ho Phi Le was born in Vietnam and came to America in 1975. He is also a self-taught photographer and since he became interested in bears and dolls his outstanding photographs have graced the pages of many publications including *Teddy Bear and friends*® and *Doll Reader*®. His work is also exemplified in his three books: *The Romance of Dolls & Teddy Bears, Forget-Me-Not* and *Angels from the Heart*, all published by Hobby House Press. He proudly poses for this picture with the first teddy bear he ever made at a teddy bear making workshop in 1993.

During one of my many research adventures to the Library of Congress in Washington D.C. I was thrilled to discover a bear representing the Smithsonian Bear (please refer to page 63, top right for picture of original) in the Museum of Natural History. It seemed only appropriate to have our photograph taken in front of the nation's Capitol.

Pictured are past presidents and members of the International League of Teddy Bear Clubs. These people have contributed so much to promoting the interests of teddy bear collecting and bringing together collectors around the world. Front row left to right: Marcia Campbell (1992, 1993 President), Jill Pearson, Gale Darter, Ken Bird (Founder and 1985, 1986 & 1987 President), (Back row left to right) Audrey West, Doris Shepherd, Sue Coe (1994 President), Pat Todd (1990, 1991 President), Mary Jo Hafner, Suzanne Irvin (1988, 1989 President).

In addition to clubs, the teddy bear world has two official prize recognition events. Each is sponsored by a magazine. *Teddy Bear and friends*® holds the annual TOBY® Awards. Thirteen categories are judged by researchers, dealers, writers, historians, editors, artists, retailers, manufacturers and museum curators. The categories include: Artist Categories, Manufacturer Categories, Teddy Bear Design Category and Special Awards.

The annual Golden Teddy Awards contest is sponsored by *Teddy Bear Review*®. This is a reader awards contest, selected from a huge field of entries honed down by a panel of five qualified judges. Main categories for the Golden Teddy Awards are: Handmade/Hobbyist, Handmade/Working Artist and Manufacturer.

There are many different opinions on how to place material value on a bear. Bears with a certain provenance, family heirlooms, childhood treasures, bears whose fur and/or condition portray generations of love (page 5, top right). These, in many cases, have more value to their owner than any bear imaginable.

This book takes a look at some special bears and their families, along with their creators and/or manufacturers. You will also find some historic perspectives of this sturdy entity. For more information and details, please refer to my earlier books listed on page 144.

Promoting Linda's San Diego Teddy Bear, Doll and Antique Toy Show and Sale since 1983 has been challenging but a very rewarding experience for me.

Three dear friends and international celebrities in the teddy bear world are guests at my teddy bear shows. Left to right are Rosemary Volpp, Pat Schoonmaker and Helen Sieverling. These gracious sharing ladies have contributed so much to the popularity of teddy bear collecting in America by their books, articles, slide presentations and travels around the world teaching collectors about the history and general information on our beloved teddy.

Top left: Donna Harrison West is a well-known face on the teddy bear circuit. She was bitten by "The Teddy Bear Bug" when she purchased her first small bear at a Pennsylvania Doll Show in 1981. She has produced more than 20 teddy bear shows in her hometown of Baltimore, Maryland, and in 1986 added a convention to her repertoire. She has co-authored *Teddy Bear Artists Annual* and *Advertising Art of Steiff* both published by Hobby House Press. These days Donna focuses on selling hand-crafted Native American jewelry carrying "the spirit of the bear", as well as perfecting her own beaded jewelry designs with a bear motif.

Top right: Old Friends Antiques, established in 1974, specializes in rare and unusual mint condition Steiff, Schuco and fine vintage American Bears. Operated by partner both in business and in life, Byron and Barbara Baldwin, Old Friends Antiques participates in teddy bear and collectible shows throughout America. The Baldwins and their two children live in Sparkes, Maryland. Barbara is pictured holding a magnificent huge glass-eyed white mohair, early Steiff bruin.

Left: Dottie Ayers, owner of a graphic arts studio and Teddy Bear store called "The Calico Teddy", writes a column for *Teddy Bear and friends®*. She has co-authored *Advertising Art of Steiff* and *Teddy Bear Artist Annual* both published by Hobby House Press. Dottie also authenticates and provides appraisals of antique bears and lectures on topics of bear collecting across the United States.

Chapter Two

The Birth of the American Teddy Bear

Native American Bear Worship

The common traditions of bear worship link great Native American tribes from coast to coast; from hunter-warriors to farmer-hunters; from North American Eskimos to South American pre-Columbian rituals, the bear has been revered and honored since time immemorial. In both the New World and the Old World, cultures celebrate the bear. Bears represent an immortal and vital part of initiation, symbolizing transformation, growth and renewal. Our view of the teddy bear is part of a natural evolution.

According to legend, Cree hunters performed bear hunting rites and rituals because it pleased the bears and made them want to be killed. Most Indian cultures, and the Cree were no exception, strongly sympathized with their game animals, and this is one reason bears were held in such deep respect early in history.

After the bear was killed, bear images were carved in various stones and worn by the hunters and their families.

Photograph of Theodore Roosevelt. Theodore Roosevelt referred to Clifford Berryman's famous cartoon character with whom he was associated as the "Berryman Bear." On January 4, 1908 the President inscribed one of his photographs to the creator of his popular associate with the following notation: "The Creator of the 'Berryman Bear' always has the call on the Roosevelt administration! My dear Mr. Berryman, you have the real artist's ability to combine great cleverness and keen truthfulness with entire freedom from malice. Good citizens are your debtors. Ever your friend, Theodore Roosevelt." Bear. Unidentified American Manufacturer. Circa 1907; 13in (33cm).

At night, the adornments were set in a fetish pot, filled with food said to give the sacrificial souls of the dead animals nourishment. The Cree believed that all beings, food animals included, are immortal...if we are to rely on our Native American ancestor's concepts, our modern behavior and the birth of the American teddy bear would bear witness to this ideology.

There are scores of books written on the subject of the bear in Native American culture and religion. One I highly recommend is *Giving Voice to the Bear*, by David Rockwell (Roberts Rinehart Publishers, 1991). This book, and others like it, will open your eyes to centuries-old human admiration for bears.

Today, the teddy bear is our modern day talisman that makes us feel good. Its nurturing qualities have grown from those early American times over the years. Modern day collectors seem to acknowledge that deep sense within their souls and honor the bear for his lasting importance in our history and well being.

Our native American ancestors were particularly devoted to the bear. Many tribes believed that all beings, particularly food animals, are immortal. Our modern behavior, the birth of the American teddy bear, and our perpetual reverence for this lovable creation bear witness to this ideology. Note the reflection in the water: the image of the bear. Pencil drawing by Gisele Nash.

The Berryman Bear

The next historic depiction of the bear in American culture is clearly a direct link to the teddy bear. Clifford Berryman, political cartoonist extraordinaire, created what was probably the most popular of all cartoon symbols, the little Berryman Bear. This bear came into being after news of President Theodore Roosevelt's refusal to shoot a defenseless captured bear during a Mississippi bear hunt (November 14, 1902). When the story reached Berryman at *The Washington Post*, the imaginative artist depicted this sportsmanlike incident on the front page (November 16, 1902) (photo at left). The public response was overwhelming. Berryman received floods of letters requesting repeats of the bear.

Theodore Roosevelt

To back track a bit, it is always interesting to look at the man most often credited with being teddy's namesake...Theodore Roosevelt. Born to a prosperous, well-established family of Dutch importers, Teedie (his family nickname) was sickly as a child. He matured to a young man who loved the great outdoors and taught himself to be an excellent horseback rider and hunting sportsman. He grew to have a great reputation as a hunter, but, in fact, he dearly loved animals and nature. His passion for hunting bear in particular was not solely to kill them, but to observe their natural habits. The grizzlies became his favorites.

People loved him. He was amusing, entertaining and always laughed loudly at his own jokes. He simply adored children and was a devoted father. His was a new type of presidential family, close and affectionate. Their activities often took precedence over affairs of state.

Through his delight in his own children, young Americans were also drawn towards the kind, chivalrous President. Perhaps he is best summed up by his great friend, Jacob A. Riis:

"Boys admire President Roosevelt because he, himself, is a good deal of a boy. Some men have claimed that Mr. Roosevelt never has matured; but this is saying no more that he has not stopped growing, that he is not yet imprisoned in the crust of age. To him the world is still young and unfinished. He has a boy's fresh faith that the things that ought to be done can be done. His eyes are on the future, rather than on the past.

"Young Americans never drew so near to any other public man as Theodore Roosevelt. All the boys in the land feel that there is a kindred spirit in the White House. Everyone of them

Top left: On November 16, 1902, Clifford K. Berryman depicted President Theodore Roosevelt's refusal to shoot a captured bear during a 1902 Mississippi bear hunt on page one of *The Washington Post* as part of a montage titled "The Passing Show." Berryman's famous cartoon symbol originated from this drawing the appealing little teddy bear. *Courtesy The Library of Congress.*

Left: Shortly after the first version of Clifford K. Berryman's famous cartoon ("Drawing the Line in Mississippi") was published in *The Washington Post* on November 16, 1902 (top left) it appears the Washington National Press Club requested the "original" of this drawing that aroused such national attention. When it became apparent the original was missing Berryman drew a second version (pictured in this illustration). This second and most publicized version of Clifford K. Berryman's famous cartoon, "Drawing the Line in Mississippi", is somewhat changed from the original. Roosevelt is drawn with the same hand in upraised position, but this time he appears as a more robust figure, his facial expression kind and forgiving. The captured bear now resembles an appealing little cub. *Courtesy Smithsonian Institute.*

Above: In the months that followed the notorious President Roosevelt hunt, we observe many changes in the shape and form of the bear Berryman drew for *The Washington Post* on November 16, 1902. In this cartoon drawn by Berryman on June 28, 1903 we see the frightened bruin in earlier cartoons has begun to evolve into an adorable little bruin. His character already taking shape by the expression the clever cartoonist has given to the bear's face. Berryman referred to his new cartoon symbol as the "Roosevelt" bear and thereafter whenever he cartooned the President, the little bear was on hand. *Courtesy from The U.S. Senate Collection, Center for Legislative Archives.*

Right: Clifford K. Berryman Cartoon: 1904, "This is Quite as Near the 'Real Thing' as I Wish to Get." Pen and Ink drawing. Berryman reportedly was the first cartoonist to portray President Theodore Roosevelt as a teddy bear. *Courtesy from the U.S. Senate Collection, Center for Legislative Archives.*

BERRYMAN AT WORK FOR YOUR ENJOYMENT
Mr. Berryman entertains nearly everybody in Washington every day with his cartoons on the first page of The Star.

Right: In 1907 Clifford Berryman left his position as chief cartoonist at *The Washington Post*, to fulfill his long ambition to work for *The Washington Evening Star*. He took with him, of course, his trademark, the lovable little teddy bear that was now internationally famous.

Left: Ideal Bears. Early 1900s; sizes (top row 9in [23cm]), bottom row left 14in (36cm) right 13in (33cm) various shades of short gold mohair; black and white "googlie" eyes; black twisted pearl cotton horizontally stitched nose; jointed arms and legs; swivel head; excelsior stuffing; torso seam closes in front; foot pads come to point. Note the similarity of the eyes glancing to the side of the plush bears to Clifford Berryman's bear depicted in this original Berryman cartoon. *Private collection. Photograph by Larry McDaniel.*

Below: (Left) Steiff "Clifford Berryman" Bear. 1987. 13in (35cm); brown mohair; white mohair in-set snout; felt-lined open mouth; black and white plastic "googlie" eyes; jointed arms and legs; swivel head; airbrushed paw pads; Steiff incised in script on large brass button; yellow cloth-weave stock label. Discontinued. To commemorate renowned cartoonist Clifford Berryman's immortal portrayal of Teddy Roosevelt's 1902 bear hunt in Mississippi, Linda Mullins, together with the Steiff company created the 85th Anniversary Clifford Berryman Bear. Center. Book. *The Teddy Bear Men: Theodore Roosevelt & Clifford Berryman* by Linda Mullins. Published by Hobby House Press, 1987. (Right) "Berryman Bear" (prototype). 1985. 14in (36cm); brown mohair, white mohair in-set snout; black and white plastic "googlie" eyes; jointed arms and legs; swivel head. Linda Mullins commissioned Flore Emory to create this "Berryman Bear" representing Clifford Berryman's famous cartoon symbol of the appealing little teddy bear.

knows 'Teddy' and the 'Teddy Bear' and the 'Teddy Hat.'...
He is 'Teddy' Roosevelt to millions of boys who delight in
their comradeship with the President which this nickname
implies. It does not mean that they are lacking in respect for
him; it ... means that they are not afraid of him, and that they
feel they know him and he knows them."

Even before that famous bear hunt, Roosevelt had been a
familiar figure in Berryman's cartoons. Because of the association with Theodore Roosevelt, the popular little bear began to make regular appearances whenever Berryman drew
the President. (When Berryman left *The Post* for *The Washington Star*, the bear went with him.) (Page 11, bottom right.)

After the "hunt," the *New York Herald* was the harbinger
of the association Roosevelt and bears would have in many
different media forms in the years to come: "President
Roosevelt had great success hunting bear at the White House
Christmas morning. He started on the trail for the library,
where the Christmas presents were assembled, and there he
found three miniature bears waiting for him." (December 28,
1902).

The day after the article appeared, the President wrote
Clifford Berryman a letter expressing his delight with the little
bear cartoons that had followed the original of the notorious
hunt. Although Roosevelt continued to call the little bruin a

Right: Due to Theodore (Teddy) Roosevelt's association with bears, numerous postcards featured bears humorously mimicking Roosevelt's image. Illustrated on this postcard (circa 1907) the bear carries the famous
Roosevelt "big stick" and under his arm is the recognizable "rough-rider"
hat. *Courtesy Susan Nicholson*

Below: A postcard designed by C. Barnes, copyrighted in 1907 by T.R.
Gaines of New York and published by Novelty Company of Rhode Island,
expressed the fear that the teddy bear craze was over with two cute poems.
Courtesy Susan Nicholson.

THE TEDDY BEAR SAYS:

Mr. President, I feel blue,
And I scarce know what to do,
For I have been told to-day
That a third term you won't stay.
Tell me quickly its absurd,
This rumor that I just have heard,
For if to run you don't agree,
My finish I can plainly see.

.Copyright 1907. by
T R. Gaines, N.Y.

THE LITTLE DOLLY SAYS:

Dear Mr. President be firm,
And don't accept a third term,
Teddy Bears for years, you know,
Have caused us dolls lots of woe,
Please don't run 'twill end this fad
And make every dolly glad.
We'll forgive the harm you've done
If you promise not to run.

A
THIRD
TERM
?

94

On the day of Theodore Roosevelt's inauguration, March 4, 1905, Berryman drew two cartoons on page one of *The Washington Post*. "The Evolution of The Roosevelt Bear" (Berryman's name for his cartoon symbol) and "The Original Roosevelt Man." The adorable Roosevelt Bear cartoon beginning with the President's capture of the bear in 1902, depicts stages of his eventful life up until Roosevelt's inauguration day. *Courtesy Library of Congress.*

Clifford K. Berryman cartoon. "Ready for the Festivities." *The Washington Post*, March 4, 1905. Uncle Sam makes himself ready for Theodore Roosevelt's Inaugural Ball. Berryman's Bear is splendidly dressed for the occasion in his smart Rough Rider outfit. *Richard Friz Collection.*

Numerous jokes and pranks were played on the good-natured President about his association with the teddy bear. One popular joke of the period went: "If Theodore is President of the United States with his clothes on what is he with his clothes off? Teddy Bare!" This amusing postcard, illustrated by "Rosy" (circa 1907) assumingly refers to this joke. *Courtesy Susan Nicholson.*

An illustration from an early 1900s *Puck* magazine "Incident of Theodore's Next Hunting Trip." Note the bear carrying the banner stating "Let Us Alone!" *Courtesy David Worland.*

An excellent array of rare and highly collectible Teddy Roosevelt buttons, campaign items and teddy bear memorabilia. *Courtesy David Worland.*

"Berryman Bear," others gave him the moniker we have come to know him by...the teddy bear.

Soon novelty makers saw the opportunity to reproduce the bear as a toy. The "teddy bear" vogue swept the nation. Practically every major American city had at least one or two teddy bear factories. This lovable furry creature had captured the hearts of little people everywhere. Never before had anything compared to the craze of the teddy bear.

Roosevelt also became internationally associated with the teddy bear toy. Roosevelt recalled another humorous example which happened during a visit to England in a letter to David Gray in 1911:

"In Cambridge, everything was more informal, and it was largely a reception by the students themselves...on my arrival they had formed in two long ranks, leaving a pathway for me to walk between them and at the final turn ... they had a teddy bear seated on the pavement with outstretched paw to greet me; and when I was given my degree in the chapel, the students had rigged a kind of pulley arrangement by which they tried to let down a very large teddy bear upon me as I took the degree..."

Roosevelt's eventful, charismatic life was celebrated in numerous books, toys and games. His distinctive facial fea-

(Left) Teddy Roosevelt soft sculptured doll by American artist Steve Isenberg. (Right) Early 1900s "googlie-eyed" Ideal bear. (10in [25cm]). *Courtesy David Worland.*

tures and robust smile often adorned dishes, postcards, trays and song sheets. His name was used to advertise groceries, patriotism and self-improvement programs. There were hundreds of Teddy Roosevelt related items but the one that proved the most popular of all time is the beloved teddy bear toy.

The credit may go to Young Americans who christened these wonderful toys, naming them after their hero, Teddy Roosevelt. As *Playthings* said: "Isn't the President the hero of every boy who longs to grow big enough to hold a gun to shoot bears and some day do just the very same things that 'Teddy' Roosevelt does? So the teddy bear was named..."

So associated did Roosevelt become with the teddy bear that the Republicans adopted the popular bear as an important and delightful symbol for the President's election campaigns. Political postcards, trays, pins and mementos of all descriptions depicted Roosevelt with his friendly little companion.

Roosevelt's 1904 declaration that he would not be a presidential candidate in 1908 sent ripples of concern through the toy industry that the teddy bear craze was over. However, his announcement made little bearing on the industry, and it appears most expected him to run. At any rate, the news media and numerous political memorabilia (dated 1907) continued to depict the President along with his well-known campaign symbol, the teddy bear (page 13, bottom).

True to his word, Roosevelt did not run for a third term in 1908. He was influential in the nomination of William H. Taft, who chose the 'possum as his campaign symbol.

During the early 1900s teddy bear craze, many items of clothing depicted teddy bears. Pictured are a pair of very rare child's rough-rider style leather gauntlets with appliqued white teddy bears holding embroidered American flags. *Courtesy David Worland.*

Diane Gard's "Rough Rider" bear, made from old Pierce Arrow car upholstery fabric. A similar version of this bear is in the Teddy Roosevelt exhibit in the Smithsonian Institute in Washington D.C. The book is a copy of *The Rough Riders* by Theodore Roosevelt. *Courtesy David Worland.*

(Right to left) "Roosevelt Bears" water pitcher by Buffalo Pottery. 1907. "Teddy Bear" playing card game by Teddy Bear Novelty Co. of Silver Springs N.Y. 1907. Teddy Roosevelt soft-sculptured doll by James Gould of Indianapolis. Pinned to Roosevelt's coat is an original 1904 Campaign Teddy lapel pin, in T.R.'s right arm is a 5in (13cm) bear by Elaine Fujita Gamble. *Courtesy David Worland.*

The Craze

Horsman's
"TEDDY BULL MOOSE"
TRADE MARK REGISTERED

A READY-MADE
DEMAND FOR IT
THE COUNTRY
OVER

———

SELLS AT SIGHT

NEW YORK HERALD
Sunday, Sep^t. 15th
SAYS:

"Teddy Bull Moose
has routed
Teddy Bear, ...
he is monarch of
all the toys."

"Can't-Break-Em" Composition Head from Plastic Model
Copyrighted 1912 by E. I. Horsman Co.

Price $8.50 Per Dozen
SEND IN YOUR ORDERS
Orders Filled in Rotation as Received

E. I. HORSMAN CO. 365 Broadway NEW YORK

This cartoon published in the Atlanta Constitution
was the origin of "Billy Possum.

"BEAT IT!
TEDDY BEAR"
BEAT IT!"

"I CAN
SEE MY
FINISH!"

"BOTH OF
YOU ARE
NATURE
FAKERS"

If "Teddy Bear" why not "Billy Possum.

COPYRIGHT APPLIED FOR

Top left: Horsman advertised a "Teddy Bull Moose" in *Playthings* 1912 magazine. The concept of this unusual toy was probably inspired by Teddy Roosevelt's Progressive (Bull Moose) Party candidacy for President (1912). Please refer to the illustration on the top right of this page for an example of the actual plush Bull Moose. *Courtesy* Playthings *magazine.*

Top right: (Left) Unmarked American Manufacturer "Bull Moose" (possibly Horsman [please refer to the illustration on the top left of this page for example of "Teddy Bull Moose" advertisement]). Circa 1912. 10in (25cm); dark brown velveteen body; brown mohair mane; brown felt antlers; black button eyes; jointed legs; swivel neck; excelsior stuffing. Probably produced during Theodore Roosevelt's second run for President (1912). Private collection. (Right) Unidentified American Manufacturer. Bear. Circa 1907; 17in (43cm); light beige medium length mohair; shoe-button eyes; black fabric nose; jointed arms and legs; swivel head; excelsior stuffing; torso seam closed in back. Note large round ears. Attached to khaki cotton shirt, is a representation of highly collectible President Theodore Roosevelt campaign buttons. *Courtesy Mimi Hiscox. Photograph by Larry McDaniel.*

Left: In this rare postcard (postmarked 1907) Taft confidently confronts Roosevelt with his new campaign symbol, Billy Possum, while the defeated looking teddy bear looks on.

Even though toy makers touted the praises of President William Taft's stuffed animal mascot for the political administration, Billy Possum, ([right] 1909; 10in [25cm]) this curious creature fell short of the magic of the old reliable teddy bear, ([Left] Ideal. 1907. 12in [31cm]). The political postcard (1909) shows Billy Possum passing the teddy bear on his way to the White House. At the bottom of the card are the words "Good Bye Teddy." Photos of Theodore Roosevelt (left) and William Taft (right) can be seen in the corners of this card. *Courtesy Barbara Lauver.*

Three Unknown American manufactured *Billy Possums*. Circa 1909. In the background are examples of *Billy Possum* postcards. *Courtesy Mimi Hiscox.*

Billy Possum

No review of the American teddy bear can by-pass a quick look at Billy Possum, Teddy's unsuccessful successor. Teddy's rival was an attempt to attach a mascot to William H. Taft, who followed Teddy Roosevelt into office. Taft's affiliation with the 'possum came to light when he ordered a meal of "'possum and 'taters" during the campaign. When he proclaimed "For 'possum first, last and all the time," the press capitalized on his speech and began to initiate use of the unattractive marsupial in many of its political drawings.

The toy industry made every effort to artificially foist Billy Possum's merits on the public, but he simply could not compete with his sweet little cousin the teddy bear. Today, Billy Possum toys and related political memorabilia are extremely rare and desirable collectors' items (pages 18, 19, and 20).

As the American public was disappointed with Billy Possum, Roosevelt was disappointed in the accomplishments of his successor, Taft. In 1912, Roosevelt threw his hat in the ring and was nominated to a new Progressive Party (Bull Moose) ticket. There was a flurry of postcard messages which included "I won't be happy till I get my teddy back." However, Woodrow Wilson benefited from the split Republican ticket and was elected over Taft and Roosevelt.

Left: Plush possums and possum memorabilia items are rare and highly collectible among bear collectors. Pictured are two desirable plush examples. (Left) Unknown American manufacturer. Circa 1909. 11in (28cm); gray variegated mohair; beige felt face; shoe-button eyes jointed arms and legs; swivel head; excelsior stuffing. Note the mohair surrounding face gives appearance of the possum wearing a fur body suit. (Right) Fisher *Billy Possum*. 10in (25cm); light gray mohair; shoe-button eyes; jointed arms and legs; swivel head; excelsior stuffing. Knitted outfit not original. (Left front) Printed fabric "Billy Possum" 5in (13cm). "Billy Possum" buttons, buckle, spoon and forks surround these amusing creatures. *Courtesy Mimi Hiscox.*

Below: These regal looking bruins were produced by Steiff around 1905. The wonderful elongated characteristics and facial appeal are the recognizable traits of these desirable bears. *Photograph by Larry McDaniel.*

Teddy Roosevelt's great accomplishments as a man and United States President will always be remembered, but the special toy he lent his name to years ago will be with us forever. We honor Roosevelt for his part in the evolution of our undaunted little friend the teddy bear, a toy that will continue to spread love, happiness and friendship throughout the country and the world.

The depth of the Roosevelt and Berryman affiliation and their individual stories so fascinated me that I made a special pilgrimage to The Library of Congress in Washington D.C. (page 6, top right). The result was an entire book on the subject of Clifford Berryman and Theodore Roosevelt entitled *The Teddy Bear Men*. If you want more details on the important role this saga plays in the development of the American teddy bear, please refer to that book!

Who Deserves the Credit?

There is much controversy surrounding the birth of the American teddy bear. Everybody likes to take credit for inventing this special creature. It is not surprising that four people are credited in their obituaries with creating the teddy bear: Clifford Berryman, Margarete Steiff, Morris Michtom and Seymour Eaton. For instance, The Ideal Toy Company (see page 60) certainly claims to be one of the first to jump on the bandwagon.

At the same time, across the ocean, the Steiff Company was creating its own version of a furry bruin (page 20, bottom). Sales of these bears began to increase. They were most probably introduced in shops in summer resort towns along the New Jersey shore (1906). In Patricia N. Schoonmaker's book, *A Collector's History of the Teddy Bear*, articles taken from *Playthings* October and November 1906 issues identify Margarete Steiff as the originator of the teddy bear. "Teddy" Roosevelt's increasing popularity and the continuation of Clifford Berryman's cartoon featuring the appealing little bear were the best promotion the Steiff bears could have.

The Roosevelt Bears of Seymour Eaton

Clifford Berryman never referred to his "dingbat" (cartoonist's symbol) as a teddy bear. He referred to it as a Roosevelt Bear. Others called it a Berryman Bear. A notable series of bear related children's books were written in the early 1900s with the same family name as the President. The Roosevelt Bears, created by Seymour Eaton (top right photo), were two huge bears. Teddy B and Teddy G

Top right: Professor Seymour Eaton pictured in *The American Course, Volume I*. Seymour Eaton is the creator of the Roosevelt Bears. *Courtesy Charles R. Moose.*

Right: The famous Roosevelt Bear books created by Paul Piper under the pen name Seymour Eaton. The first book, *The Roosevelt Bears, Their Travels and Adventures*, was published in 1905. Three more books in this series followed: *More About the Roosevelt Bears* (1906), *The Roosevelt Bears Abroad* (1907), and *The Bear Detectives* (1907) published by Edward Stern & Company, Inc., Philadelphia. Hardback cover is 8in (22cm) by 11in (29cm). The follow-up series to the first four volumes of the *Roosevelt Bears* book by Seymour Eaton were small editions with fewer colored plates.

Front and back cover of the booklet *The Teddy Bear's Baking School*. Copyright 1906-1907 Seymour Eaton and Edward Stern & Co., Inc. The summer of 1907 Fleischmann Co. distributed this complementary twelve-page booklet with colored covers. In this story, Teddy B. and Teddy G. taught nursery rhyme characters to bake, with extensive praise for Fleischmann's yeast. *Courtesy Thelma Kimble.*

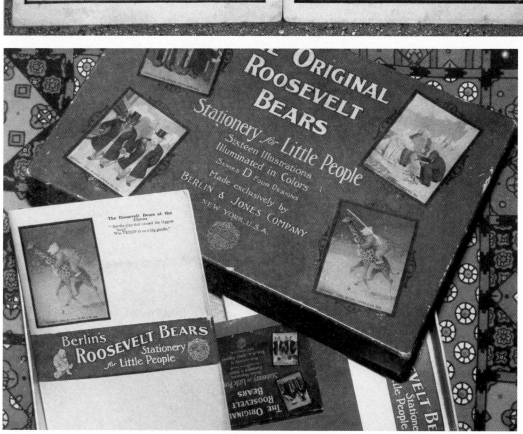

Rare illustrated boxed set of children's stationery. "The Original Roosevelt Bears" writing paper features the adventurous Roosevelt Bears (illustrated by V. Floyd Campbell) and tiny envelopes. Copyright Edward Stern 1906. Made by Berlin and Jones Company New York, USA. *Courtesy David Worland.*

(B for black and G for gray...not bad and good as some people think) look more like real bears than Teddies (top illustration), but their influence on the toy bear market was tremendous.

Initially a district school teacher, Eaton used the pseudonym Paul Piper when penning his first work of fiction (1904), a charming short story, which received complimentary reviews.

In 1905, Eaton began the famous series of children's stories still popular today. They were first illustrated by V. Floyd Campbell, until his death. Each episode told of an adventure of the two bears on their travels to the East and was designed to fit on one full newspaper page.

The *New York Times* began advertising the series on January 3, 1906, crediting authorship to the pen name "Paul Piper," but after the series was a proven success, Eaton rightfully claimed his creation once more.

Most papers ran the series on Sundays, with evening papers running the stories on Saturday. It ran for 29 weeks (concluding on July 31, 1906). The timing was perfect. Roosevelt was at the height of popularity. In February, the wedding of his daughter Alice was an international social event. The day after she was wed, the episode "The Bears in a Balloon" shared the edition reporting the wedding.

In the 20th episode, R.K. Culver replaced Campbell as the illustrator with no apparent change in style.

By June 1906, the Bronx zoo had two bear cubs from Colorado which were named Teddy B and Teddy G.

In August, *The New York Times* showed children's drawings of "Mrs. Bear taking her baby bear in its go-cart for an airing." Two weeks later it reported on fashionable women who carried stuffed toy bears on the beach. By the fall, the fad moved into the cities and the term "Roosevelt Bears, Teddy B. and Teddy G." was shortened to teddy bears, according to research by Charles R. Moose in his article "The Naming of the Teddy Bear," *Teddy Bear and friends*®, May/June 1990.

Moose also reports that in November of the same year *The Washington Post* observed that "Teddy Bears Forced out the Doll," and identified Margarete Steiff as the originator.

That fall, the first 18 episodes from Eaton's well-read serial were published in book form: *The Roosevelt Bears—Their Travels and Adventures*. The second series of 18 stories called *The Roosevelt Bears Abroad* started up in February 1907. By the third installment, the name "teddy bears" started to emerge.

Then another book called *More About Teddy B. and Teddy G., The Roosevelt Bears* came out. Both Campbell and Culver illustrations were used, as well as four new chapters all using the term "teddy bears." Charles Moose's scholarly research again shows us that there is a picture of the Roosevelt bears returning home to Colorado with a jointed teddy bear as a gift.

Their third Roosevelt Bears book was based on the 1907 series and published the next year. It had 18 stories and 16 full-color illustrations. A fourth book, *The Bear Detectives*, was based on a third newspaper series which began in October 1907.

In addition to Charles Moose, Pat Schoonmaker (*A Collector's History of the Teddy Bear*) also recognized in 1979, Eaton's important role in naming the teddy bear.

(Please refer to Chapter Five, "Advertising Bears" for more information on the importance of the media in placing teddy bears in the forefront of the American Scene.)

Pages from the *Nashville Banner* (May 1907), showing three installments of Seymour Eaton's "The Roosevelt Bears Abroad." Illustrations by R.K. Culver. *Courtesy David Worland.*

The Teddy Bear and the Doll at Christmas

How to Dress Them: By Ida Cleve Van Auken

Evidence of the influence of Seymour Eaton's Roosevelt Bears can be found not only in ads referring to the bears as Teddy B. and Teddy G., but these names were also embroidered on Teddy Bear clothes. This *Ladies Home Journal* 1907 advertisement pictured teddy bear outfits consisting of Pajama suit, Rough Rider suit, Playsuit (top of page), Fireman's suit, Sailor suit and Clown suit (bottom of page). Note several outfits are monogrammed with either "Teddy B" or "Teddy G."

Bear by American artist Jeanette Warner. (15in [38cm]) wears a pair of circa 1907 "Teddy B" overalls. The milk glass candy container in the form of a travel case depicts the Roosevelt bears. The 1910 bear bank (right) was produced by the Arcade Mfg. Co., Freeport, Ill. *Courtesy David Worland.*

Early American Teddy Bear Manufacturers

It didn't take long for the endearing term, "teddy bear", to become a household name. In April of 1906, *Playthings* magazine (founded in 1903), published the first known national advertisement for American teddy bears. Baker and Bigler Co. (New York) presented an ad picturing a jointed teddy bear. The headline read "This is Bruin's Day," and continuing copy displayed "The American Line of Jointed Plush Bears." (Photo below.) Early advertisements referred to the new toy as bruins, or just simply, bears.

The next issue, May 1906 *Playthings*, published an ad which appears to be the first documented use of the words "Teddy's Bears" (when referring to the toy bear) in print. (Page 25, top right.)

By July of the same year, Kahn and Mossbacher were advertising Teddy B and Teddy G clothes for bears in the popular toy magazine. In an October 1906 article in *Playthings*, bears were still referred to as "Bruins" ("All for Dear Bruin"). Also, in this same issue was the article "When Bears Go Motoring." Here *Playthings* used the term "Teddy Bear." This was apparently the very first time a national publication dropped the apostrophe "s" from the nomenclature and "Teddy" became the official name of the stuffed bear. However, in an article ("The Plush Bear Craze") in *Playthings* next issue, (November 1906), the terms *bruin, Teddy's Bears* and *Teddy bear* were used. This appears to be the transitional period for the name.

Just six months after Baker and Bigler's advertisement, the term "teddy bear" was fully established across America.

By 1908, the toy industry began to question the future or the fate of the teddy bear. Could this incredible fad continue at this pace? We all know the answer was a thundering YES. Teddy bears were proving to be truly the most loved toy of all time.

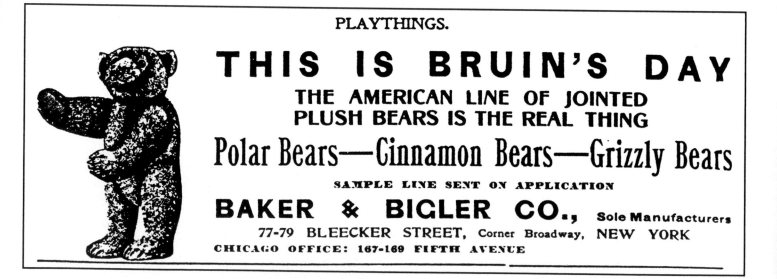

The first known advertisement for jointed plush bears in a national American magazine-April 1906 *Playthings* magazine. Note: no mention as yet of the bears being called "Teddy Bears," just "Bruins" or simply bears. *Courtesy* Playthings.

More than twenty companies were making teddy bears in the United States alone. The teddy bear craze was not just confined to children. Even though it began with youngsters, the spell of the cuddly new toy was quick to capture adults as well.

The early 20th Century saw a wide variety of teddy bear designs coming forth. Everything imaginable depicted teddy's image: torsos of bears concealed music boxes, self-whistling devices (page 31, top right) and candy containers. An extremely popular bear still highly sought after today, was the electric eye bear. Various methods were developed to light-up teddy's eyes. (Page 42, bottom left and right; page 43, bottom right.)

Dolls still dominated the market and some innovations included jointed teddy bear bodies combined with bisque, celluloid or composition doll faces. (Page 46, bottom left; page 47, top left.)

Enterprising manufacturers produced complete outfits for the bears (page 23, bottom right) and patterns for ambitious mothers to use in sewing teddy bear clothes for their children were available as well. Like dolls, teddies enjoyed having their own toys to ride around in. Wagons, circus carts, and cages were products advertised by Lloyd Manufacturing Company (Menominee, Michigan) and Hamburger and Co. made pedal cars for life-size teddies to drive.

When advertising their product, a sizable number of the plush teddy bear manufacturers would state that the quality of their bears were "equal to the imported", referring to their German counterparts. In my estimation, this proves to be true. Bears made by Aetna, Bruin Manufacturing Company, Ideal and Hecla (see page 25, bottom right; page 27, top right; page 29, top right; page 60, bottom) are perfect examples of the manufacturers choice of high grade mohair fabric and beautiful design.

It is difficult to attribute a definite style to the American Bear. However, several features were used more commonly on domestic bears manufactured by less prestigious companies. For example, American style bodies were longer and narrower than their German counterparts. The long arms and curved paws were changed to short arms with less, or in some cases, hardly any curve to the paw at all. Feet were also smaller by comparison, and the legs were very straight. (Page 42, top left; page 53, bottom right.)

The head and nose were not accentuated like those of the Germans. Their construction and jointing method was not changed though, and mohair and excelsior were primarily used.

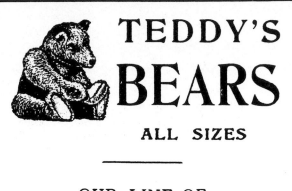

Top right: This E.I. Horsman advertisement ran in *Playthings* September 1906 issue, was the very first time (in *Playthings*) that bears were called teddy bears, actually "Teddy's Bears." *Courtesy* Playthings.

Right: Aetna. Bear. Circa 1910. 20in (51cm); light beige mohair; glass eyes; fully jointed; excelsior stuffing. Note shape of head, position of ears, fairly long silky mohair, and cardboard underlies the felt "flat" foot pads, all are characteristics of Aetna. *Courtesy Mort and Evelyn Wood.*

Three features seem to stick out: extremely firm stuffing, short, bristly mohair and low grade felt paw pads. (Page 54, top left.)

This chapter is designed to give you a pictorial representation of early American teddy bears, along with information regarding their characteristics. To the best of my knowledge, I've approximated the appropriate time frame of each bear. Extensive study of early 20th century advertisements, numerous bears and the interchange of sharing information with a knowledgeable network of bear dealers and collectors has made it possible to associate certain characteristics to specific manufacturers.

Unfortunately, there were a great number of American bears that were not identified with any permanent manufacturers mark, nor have advertisements surfaced to aid us in the identification of "mystery" bears. Over the years I have become more confident

Example of the different characteristics and facial features of three highly collectible early 1900s American bears. (Left to right) Aetna. Circa 1907. 20in (51cm); rich silky cinnamon-colored mohair; glass eyes; fully jointed; excelsior stuffing; cardboard lined foot pads; (originally "AETNA" was stamped on right foot pad). Note high placement of ears, shape of head, eye placement and cardboard lined foot pads are this company's traits. Center. Ideal. Circa 1907. 14in (36cm); golden colored mohair; shoe-button eyes; fully jointed; excelsior stuffing. Note triangular shaped head, round low-set ears and eyes set close together, identifies this bear as Ideal. (Right) Bruin Manufacturing Company (B.M.C.). Circa 1907. 16in (41cm); white silky mohair; glass eyes; light brown stitched nose, mouth and claws; fully jointed; excelsior and kapok stuffing; woven label on foot reads: "B.M.C." *Courtesy Barbara Baldwin.*

These early 1900s American teddy bears represent the quality produced by three domestic manufacturers. (Left to right) Aetna. Circa 1907. 20in (51cm); dense pinkish beige mohair; glass eyes; jointed arms and legs; swivel head; excelsior stuffing; stamped on foot "AETNA." (Center) Ideal. Circa 1907. 18in (46cm); off-white mohair; shoe-button eyes; jointed arms and legs; swivel head; excelsior stuffing. (Right) Unidentified American manufacturer. Circa 1907. 16in (41cm); honey gold mohair; shoe-button eyes; jointed arms and legs; swivel head; excelsior stuffing. *Courtesy Barbara Baldwin.*

Right: Bruin Manufacturing Co. (B.M.C.) Bear. Circa 1907. 14in (36cm); silky apricot-colored mohair; glass eyes; fully jointed; excellsior and kapok stuffing; woven label on foot reads "B.M.C." It appears that the Bruin Mfg. Company was only in business for approximately one year. So these beautiful examples of a quality American bear are extremely rare. If the label of the bear has been removed, identifying features are high grade silky mohair, eyes were glass, stuffing was soft using a lot of cotton and kapok. The arms are curved but not elongated. *Courtesy Barbara Baldwin.*

Below left: Bruin Manufacturing Co. (B.M.C.) Bear. Circa 1907; 14in (36cm); silky white mohair; glass eyes; fully jointed; excelsior stuffing; woven label on foot reads: "B.M.C." Note the characteristics and quality mohair is very similar to the German-made imports. Bruin advertised "'Trademark: B.M.C.' Look for the label, every piece carries our trademark in gold letters. The only featherweight line on the market. B.M.C. stamped on foot." *Courtesy Karen Silverstein. Photograph by Joan Sage.*

Below right: (Front) Bruin Manufacturing Co. (B.M.C.) Circa 1907. 14in (36cm); honey-colored mohair; shoe-button eyes; jointed arms and legs; swivel head; excelsior stuffing. Woven silk label on right foot reads; "B.M.C." (Top) Unidentified American manufacturer. Circa 1908. 9in (23cm); blonde mohair; shoe-button eyes; jointed arms and legs; swivel head; excelsior stuffing. Bear seated on early 1900s drum decorated with dressed bears. *Courtesy Mimi Hiscox.*

Left: Columbia Mfg. Co. Laughing Roosevelt Bear. Circa 1907. 16in (41cm); short gold mohair; glass eyes; composition open mouth with two milk glass teeth; jointed arms and legs; small paws and feet; low grade wool felt paw pads; swivel head; excelsior stuffing. Mouth opens and closes when tummy is pressed. A Roosevelt Laughing Teddy Bear was advertised by the Columbia Teddy Bear Manufacturers in *Playthings* 1907 magazine. "The Laughing Teddy Bear Laughs and Shows his Teeth at tight money, hard times and pessimists." (Referring to Teddy Roosevelt's philosophies). *Courtesy Barbara Lauver.*

Below: Unmarked American manufacturer. Possibly Harman Mfg. Co., New York. Bear. Circa 1910. Approximate size 26in (66cm); honey-colored mohair; glass eyes; "inset fabric" nose; jointed arms and legs; swivel head; excelsior stuffing. Note wide head. *Courtesy Barbara Lauver.*

in the documentation of certain bears as being "Made in America." The trails which lead to these conclusions are shared with you in the captions below each illustration.

I have always been an avid collector of Steiff bears. However, since researching the American bears for this book, I discovered that I am fascinated by the variety of design, the facial expressions and the appeal of the body characteristics of these domestic creations. The Steiff bears are magnificent —and — for the most part far over shadow their early American counterparts. However, you may be drawn to add these special bears pictured here to your collections. Not only will their presence enhance your display...but may just bring a smile to your face!

For a detailed catalogue of American Bear Manufacturers, please refer to my book, *Teddy Bears Past & Present/Volume Two.* Here you will find a list of each American Teddy Bear manufacturer and its particular characteristics and products.

Right: Hecla Bear. Circa 1907. 13in (33cm); creamy white mohair; clear glass eyes; "rust"-colored cotton stitched nose, mouth and claws; jointed arms and legs; swivel head; excelsior stuffing. Characteristic of Hecla is the rust colored stitching for features. *Courtesy Barbara Lauver.*

Below: Hecla Bear. Circa 1907. 16in (41cm); long, silky white mohair; shoe-button eyes; "rust cotton thread" stitched nose (vertically stitched), mouth and claws; jointed arms and legs; swivel head; excelsior stuffing. Appealing face with nice curve to paws and large feet. Note: rust colored stitched nose, mouth & claws appears to be an identifying trait of Hecla. Beautiful elongated body features resemble the early Steiff design. *Courtesy Robert Welch.*

Left: Unmarked American Manufacturer (possibly Miller Mfg. Co.). Bear. Circa 1907. 14in (36cm); black "wooly" mohair; black button eyes; jointed arms and legs; swivel head; excelsior stuffing. Extremely rare color. Magnificent elongated snout, paws and feet. Characteristics attributable to Miller Mfg. Co. This company also advertised "black" mohair bears in a *Playthings* 1907 magazine advertisement. *Courtesy Barbara Baldwin.*

Below: The Strauss Company advertised their "Self-Whistling Bear" on postcards (1907). The whistling mechanism for this American made toy is encased in the torso. (Please refer to page 31, top left). Strauss also advertised a *Musical Bear* and a *Teddy, The Organ Grinder. Courtesy Susan Nicholson.*

The whistling mechanism found in the Strauss "Self-Whistling Bear," (pictured). A brass cylinder sealed with lead at each end contains the whistling mechanism. Whistling sound is produced by turning the bear upside down and right side up again. (Please refer to page 30, bottom right and this page, top right for additional examples of self-whistling bears). *Courtesy Martha and Jim Hession.*

(Left) Strauss "Self-Whistling" bear. Circa 1907. 18in (46cm); white mohair; shoe-button eyes; rust pearl cotton stitched nose, mouth and claws; jointed arms and legs; swivel head; excelsior stuffing; whistling mechanism is encased in body. Strauss Mfg. Co. of New York advertised in *Playthings* 1907 magazine a "Self-Whistling Teddy Bear" who whistled as he was turned upside down and right side up again. Characteristic of Strauss bears are leather paw pads, and bright rust stitched facial features and claws. (Right) Columbia Teddy Bear Manufacturer. Laughing Roosevelt Bear. 1907. 20in (51cm); short orangy-gold colored mohair; glass eyes; composition open mouth with milk glass teeth (mouth opens when tummy is pressed); jointed arms and legs; swivel head; excelsior stuffing.

(Left) Unidentified American Manufacturer. Bear. Circa 1908. 17in (43cm); medium length white mohair; black button eyes; black twisted pearl cotton stitched nose (vertically stitched); jointed arms and legs; swivel head; excelsior stuffing; seam closed in front of torso. Courtesy Mimi Hiscox. (Right) Unidentified American Manufacturer. Bear. Circa 1908. 15in (38cm); light golden tan mohair; black button eyes; black thin cotton stitched nose (horizontally stitched); jointed arms and legs; swivel head; excelsior stuffing; torso seam closed in back. *Private collection. Photograph by Larry McDaniel.*

Unknown American Manufacturer. Bear. Circa 1906. 18in (46cm); beige mohair; shoe-button eyes; jointed arms and legs; swivel head; excelsior stuffing; suede paw pads. (Right) Unknown American Manufacturer. Bear. Circa 1908. 18in (46cm); beige mohair; shoe-button eyes; jointed arms and legs; swivel head; excelsior stuffing. *Courtesy Mort and Evelyn Wood.*

(Left) Unidentified American Manufacturer. Bear. Circa 1908; 18in (46cm); long silky blonde mohair; shoe-button eyes; jointed arms and legs; swivel head; excelsior stuffing. Note large round low-set ears; head positioned forward on torso; rather large round snout; high pronounced hump on back; arms positioned high on body; long curved arms; large feet, narrow ankles. *Private Collection.* (Right) Unidentified American Manufacturer. Bear. Circa 1908; 19in (48cm); long silky pale gold mohair; flat black button eyes; woven silk fabric nose; jointed arms and legs; swivel head; excelsior stuffing. Note large round high-set ears; head positioned extremely forward on torso; high pronounced large hump on back; arms positioned low on body; long curved arms; large feet. *Courtesy Mimi Hiscox. Photograph by Larry McDaniel.*

The highly collectible and rare 1907 *The Busy Bears* books (left) and postcards feature the mischievous adventures throughout the days of the week of a family of bears. Published by J.I. Austen Co., with verses written by George W. Gunn, events and happenings are colorfully illustrated. Note the resemblance of the young bear in the center of the illustration from the book, to the circa 1907, 13in (33cm); honey-colored mohair bear to the right of the book. The triangular downward looking shaped head and the turned in feet (feet are designed to turn inwards) is an indication the bear was probably inspired by The Busy Bear characters.

It is the whimsical look of many early 1900s American bears that give them that special appeal. Note the large low ears and close together eyes. Dressed in an old knitted sweater (possibly original); he looks really great positioned with his arm in an old child's tool box. *Photograph by Larry McDaniel.*

Left: Unidentified American manufacturer. Bears. Circa 1908. Left, 19in (48cm), right, 14in (36cm); long silky honey colored mohair; glass eyes; brown fabric underlines black silk stitched nose (vertically stitched) (left); black stitched nose (right); black silk stitched mouth and claws (five on each paw); jointed arms and legs; swivel head; felt foot pads lined with cardboard; body stuffed with fine shaved white excelsior, mohair scraps and horsehair (mainly found in front of torso). Note large round ears, pointy hump and narrow ankles. *Courtesy Martha and Jim Hession.*

Below: (Left) Unidentified American manufacturer. Bear. Circa 1910. 22in (56cm); pale golden beige short bristle-type mohair; shoe-button eyes; large stitched (horizontal) black wool nose; stitched black wool "smiling" mouth and claws; jointed arms and legs; swivel head; excelsior stuffing. Note rather large head and full snout. (Right) Unidentified American manufacturer. Bear. Circa 1910. 24in (61cm); short gold bristle-type mohair; shoe-button eyes; black pearl cotton (not twisted) nose, mouth and claws; jointed arms and legs; swivel head; excelsior (course chunks) stuffing; shirt cuffs with handmade button holes also used for stuffing in torso. Note the round, low-positioned ears, long, straight body, arms positioned low on body. *Courtesy Martha and Jim Hession.*

Unidentified American manufacturer. Circa 1907. 18in (46cm); long, silvery white mohair; gold (color painted on back) glass eyes; rust-colored twisted pearl cotton stitched nose (stitching vertical and wide), mouth and claws (five on each paw); jointed arms and legs; swivel head; excelsior and cotton stuffing. Note large cupped ears positioned low on head similar to early Ideal bears. Arms are very wide at top. *Courtesy Martha and Jim Hession.*

Two magnificent examples of the quality and appeal American teddy bear companies produced in the early 1900s. (Left) 16in (41cm); silky blonde mohair; shoe-button eyes. (Right) 12in (31cm); rich cinnamon mohair; glass eyes. *Courtesy Barbara Baldwin.*

(Left) Unknown American manufacturer. Bear. Circa 1907. 12in (31cm); short honey-colored mohair; shoe-button eyes; cotton rust-colored stitched nose (horizontally stitched) and claws; jointed arms and legs; swivel head; excelsior stuffing. Low, fairly round ears, high hump on back and head set low on torso (no neck) is a typical American design. (Right) Unknown American manufacturer. Bear. Circa 1907. 14in (36cm); grayish beige mohair; shoe-button eyes (set close together); black "fabric" nose; jointed arms and legs; swivel head; excelsior stuffing. (Center) Coin-operated mechanical singing bird in cage. Circa 1900s. 23in (58cm) tall. *Photograph by Larry McDaniel.*

Playtime Mfg. Co. Bear head displayed on Victorian ball. Circa 1908. 10in (25cm); gold mohair head; shoe-button eyes. Beautiful colored pictures of children surround the ball. Lace and pink satin ribbon collar. Printed on felt base "Playtime Mfg. Co." *Courtesy Barbara Baldwin.*

(Left) Unmarked American manufacturer (probably Ideal). Bear. Circa 1914. 25in (64cm); short bristle-type gold mohair; glass eyes; brown fabric twill nose; fairly small ears; short slender slightly curved jointed arms; slender jointed legs with small feet; foot pads (thin felt) come to a point; no claws on paw and foot pads; long slender torso; swivel head; excelsior stuffing. (Right) Unidentified American manufacturer. Bear. Circa 1908. 21in (53cm); short bristle-type gold mohair; shoe-button eyes; brown twisted pearl cotton stitched nose (horizontally stitched), and mouth (no stitched claws); jointed arms and legs; swivel head; excelsior stuffing. Note overall round shape to head and body. Round shaped ears are sewn low on side of head. Fat upper arm tapering with slight curve to paw. Arms are positioned low on torso. Felt paws are replaced. Remains of original gold felt can be seen on foot pad. *Courtesy Martha and Jim Hession.*

(Back row left to right) American bear. (possibly Ideal). Circa 1915. 20in (51cm). Unidentified American Manufacturer. Bear. Circa 1907. 18in (46cm). American bear. (Possibly "American Toy and Mfg. Co., "White House Teddy Bears.") Circa 1907. 18in (46cm). The eyes are attached to a disk (same diameter as the disk in the neck) placed just above the disk for the neck joint. (Front row left to right) Hecla bear. Circa 1912. 18in (46cm). Ideal bear. Circa 1907. 9in (23cm). Accessories and decorations for this patriotic scene include: Background: A 19th century coverlet, double-woven linen/wool; "Lover's Knott" pattern; Book - *The Teddy Bear ABC* Copyright 1907. Sheet Music; "The Big Stick. The American Military March Two-Step. Respectfully dedicated to Theodore Roosevelt, our next president." Copyright 1910. *Courtesy Fielding Antiques (trunk) Private collection (bears). Photograph by E. Kenneth Fielding.*

(Back left to right) Columbia Teddy Bear Manufacturers. Bear. Circa 1907. 18in (46cm). Unidentified American manufacturer. "Electric-eye" Bear. Circa 1915. 24in (61cm). Eyes light up when switch affixed to back of head is turned on. Unidentified American manufacturer. Bear. Circa 1920. 10in (25cm). Unidentified American manufacturer. "Electric-eye" Bear. Circa 1915. 18in (46cm). Eyes light up when area on back of bear is pressed. Unidentified American manufacturer. Bear. Circa 1930. 4in (12cm). Wire jointed. Original owner purchased bear from Woolworth for 10 cents around 1930. (Front row left to right) Unidentified American manufacturer. "Electric-eye" Bear. Circa 1915. 13in (34cm). Eyes light up when switch encased in left ear is turned on. Unidentified American manufacturer. Walking bear on all fours. Circa 1915. 8in (22cm) long by 6in (15cm) tall. Steiff cat. Circa 1914. 9in (23cm). Unidentified American manufacturer. "Tumbling" Bear. Circa 1920. 10in (27cm). Sheet music: "Bessie and her Little Brown Bear." Circa 1906. Books: *The Teddy Bears*. Circa 1907. The Busy Bears Circa 1907. *Private collection. Photograph by E. Kenneth Fielding*

(Left to right) Unidentified American manufacturer. Bear. Circa 1910. 25in (64cm); gold mohair head, paws and feet; black fabric nose; gray cloth body, arms and legs; shoe-button eyes; jointed arms and legs (exposed joints); excelsior stuffing (body); crushed cork stuffing (head). Unidentified American manufacturer. Bear. Circa 1907. 12in (31cm); dense tan mohair; shoe-button eyes; jointed arms and legs; swivel head; kapok stuffing. Unidentified American manufacturer. Bear. Circa 1907. 12in (31cm); beige mohair; shoe-button eyes; jointed arms and legs; swivel head; excelsior stuffing. Early 1900s German bisque doll. *Private collection (bears). Fielding Antiques (toys). Photograph by E. Kenneth Fielding.*

(Right) Unidentified American manufacturer. Bear. Circa. 1925; 28in (71cm); bright gold mohair; glass stick pin eyes; ears "sliced" into head; jointed arms and legs; swivel head; excelsior stuffing. (Left) Unidentified American manufacturer. Bear. Circa 1930; 16in (41cm); bright gold short mohair; glass eyes; excelsior stuffing. This type of inexpensive bear was sold by mail order houses such as Sears and Montgomery Ward. A wonderful array of early 1900s *Goldilocks and the Three Bears* books and a mohair duck and cat surround the bears. *Private collection. Photograph by E. Kenneth Fielding.*

(Front left and right) Unidentified American manufacturer. Bears. Circa 1925. (Left) 7in (19cm); (Right) 11in (29cm); gold fabric head; felt body (an integral part of body); felt feet; glass stick pin eyes; "wire" jointed arms and legs; stationary head; excelsior stuffing. (Back left to right) Unidentified American manufacturer. Bear. Circa 1930. 9in (23cm); short gold mohair; glass eyes; "wire" jointed arms and legs; swivel head; excelsior stuffing. Unidentified American manufacturer. Bear. Circa 1920. 9in (24cm); bright gold mohair; glass eyes; jointed arms and legs; swivel head; (unusual head design, seam down center of face, seam from ear to ear). Unidentified American manufacturer. Bear. Circa 1920. 11in (28cm); white mohair; shoe-button eyes; jointed arms and legs; swivel head (rather flat face); sliced-in ears; excelsior stuffing. Dogs and cat are mohair produced around 1930. *Courtesy Fielding Antiques (swing). Private collection (bears). Photograph by E. Kenneth Fielding.*

These two early 1900s American bears have whimsical charm appealingly seated by a 1910 hand-painted palet clock. Note the bear on the left has a rust-colored velvet nose, and matching rust-colored stitched mouth and claws and beige velveteen paw pads. The low-placed ears give the white bear on the right a very naive look. Both bears are made of high quality mohair with shoe-button eyes.

(Left) Unidentified American manufacturer. Bear. Circa 1908. 14in (36cm); honey-colored short mohair; black button eyes; black silk (not twisted) stitched nose (vertically stitched), mouth and claws (three on each paw); jointed arms and legs; swivel head. Note pointy hump on back; head position forward on body. (Right) Unidentified American manufacturer. Bear. Circa 1908. 15in (38cm); light beige mohair; black button eyes; black silk (not twisted) stitched nose (vertically stitched), mouth and claws (three on each paw); jointed arms and legs; swivel head. Both bears have nice body lines more similar to German designs than the majority of American bears. *Courtesy Martha and Jim Hession.*

Early 1900s American plush bear and cloth dolls complement each other when displayed as this adorable trio are seated in an old rocking chair. *Courtesy Sherryl Shirran.*

Displaying the bears, (Unidentified American manufacturers. Circa 1907. Sizes 10in [25cm] to 15in [38cm]) dolls and fun accessories make interesting scenes, giving them character and even more appeal. *Courtesy Flore Emory (dolls, furniture and accessories), Mimi Hiscox (two bears left of the picture). Photograph by Larry McDaniel.*

41

Left: Two typical domestic style early 1900s bears. Long narrow torsos and slender arms and legs look especially charming if you choose to dress your bears in antique doll clothes as shown. *Courtesy Sherryl Shirran.*

Below left: (Left) Unidentified American manufacturer. "Electric-Eye" Bear. Circa 1907. 22in (56cm); red, white and blue mohair; eyes are small flat bulbs; jointed arms; stationary head and legs; excelsior stuffing. Eyes light up by pressing button in back of upper torso. (Right) Unidentified American manufacturer "Electric-Eye" Bear. Circa 1907. 21in (53cm); tan-colored mohair; brown fabric nose; eyes are small flat bulbs; jointed arms and legs; swivel head; excelsior stuffing. Eyes light up by pressing button on side of torso. The majority of electric-eye bears were unjointed, therefore, this jointed version is desirable. *Courtesy Sherryl Shirran.*

Below right: Unidentified American manufacturer. "Electric-Eye" Bear. Circa 1907. 16in (41cm); honey-colored mohair; glass bulb eyes; jointed arms and legs; swivel head; squeezing tummy activates battery (concealed in torso) causing eyes to light up. *Courtesy Mimi Hiscox.*

Right: (Left) Unidentified American manufacturer. Bear. Circa 1910. 14in (36cm); short blonde bristle-type mohair; black button eyes; fine black silk-stitched nose (vertically stitched), mouth and claws; jointed arms and legs; swivel head; excelsior stuffing. Note how the claws are fanned around paw. (Right) Unidentified American manufacturer. Bear. Circa 1910. 13in (33cm); long silky cinnamon-colored mohair; shoe-button eyes; black twisted pearl cotton stitched nose (horizontally stitched), mouth and claws; jointed arms and legs; (cardboard lined foot pads), swivel head; excelsior and "horsehair" stuffing. Note round head and short round body gives a baby-bear look. *Courtesy Martha and Jim Hession.*

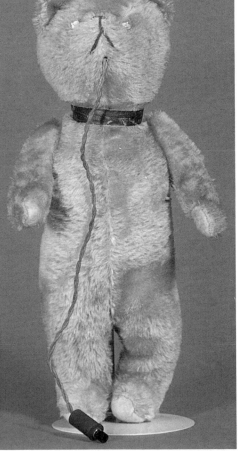

Above: These early 1900s American bears are having fun riding the vintage horse tricycle. *Courtesy Sherryl Shirran.*

Right: Unknown American manufacturer. Electric-Eye Bear. Circa 1907. 17in (43cm); short golden brown mohair; eyes are glass bulbs; jointed arms; stationary legs and head; excelsior stuffing. Eyes light up by depressing the external switch at the end of the cord which is attached to head. The external switch was more prevalent as this avoided paying patent rights for the internal switch. *Courtesy Wisconsin River Collection.*

Left: Many American electric-eye bears were designed with stationary legs and heads and produced in vivid colors. It appears these bears were introduced and became popular around 1907. *Courtesy Dottie Ayers.*

Below left: Unknown American Manufacturer. Bear. Circa 1907. 10in (25cm); short bristle-type blonde mohair (mohair covers paper mâché formed head); open mouth with formed teeth; gutta percha (hard resin) nose; glass eyes; jointed arms and legs; swivel head; excelsior stuffing. *Courtesy Wisconsin River Collection.*

Below right: My niece Carly Parris affectionately holds her favorite doll and bear from my antique doll and bear collection. (Left) P.F. Volland Raggedy Ann. Circa 1920. (Right) American teddy bear. Circa 1910.

In 1991 teddy bear artist Flore Emory's collecting interests began to include dolls. After joining a local doll club it wasn't long before beautiful dolls began to sneak into her teddy bear displays. Bears. American. Circa 1915. Dolls. Reproduction German googlie-eyed, by doll artist Gordona Little. *Photograph by Larry McDaniel.*

The bears (unidentified American manufacturers) have fun modeling the Victorian hats. (Left to right) Circa 1907. 14in (36cm); medium length light cinnamon colored mohair; shoe-button eyes; brown velveteen nose; rust colored felt mouth; rust colored stitched cotton claws; velveteen paw pads; excelsior stuffing; torso seam closes in front. Circa 1915; 16in (41cm); short bristle-type pale gold mohair; glass eyes; black twisted pearl cotton horizontally stitched nose; cotton twill paw pads; excelsior stuffing; one-piece body, "only" torso seam (closes in front). Circa 1915; 12in (31cm); short bright gold bristle-type mohair; glass eyes; black cotton vertically stitched nose; jointed arms and legs; swivel head; excelsior stuffing; torso seam closes in front; gold felt paw pads. Note slim body, arms, legs and small round feet.

Left: (Left) Unidentified American manufacturer. Bear. Circa 1915. Short golden mohair; shoe-button eyes; fabric nose; jointed arms and legs; swivel head; excelsior stuffing. (Right) Unidentified American manufacturer. Bear. Circa 1908. 20in (51cm); blonde silky mohair; black button eyes; rust-stitched nose, (horizontally stitched) mouth and claws; jointed arms and legs; swivel head; excelsior stuffing. Note large round head, ears, fairly short snout, elongated arms and feet. *Courtesy Sherryl Shirran.*

Below left: A distinctive novelty when introduced in America around 1908 was the teddy doll or Eskimo doll. They had all the features of a teddy bear body but the doll face was either celluloid composition or bisque. Usually a little hood made of the same material as the body surrounded the head. It appears by the advertisements in *Playthings* the primary manufacturers of these special creations was Hahn & Amberg, New York, and Harman Mfg. Co., New York. However, pictured at the top of the picture is a teddy doll muff with the original label that reads: "Ideal Baby Mine/U.S. Pat. Doll Muff. No 41179/I.N.C.O." *Courtesy Dot Gillett.*

Below right: The Strobel & Wilken Co. advertised Arctic Explorers "Peary" and "Cook" Eskimo Dolls produced in celebration of Peary and Cook's Arctic Exposition. *Courtesy* Playthings *magazine 1909.*

Teddy Dolls. (Left) Horsman. "Baby Bumps." Circa 1911. 11in (28cm); composition head; hand-painted facial features and hair; deep brownish gold velveteen body; jointed arms and legs; swivel head; excelsior stuffing. (Right) A. Steinhardt & Bros. "Teddy Junior." Circa 1910. 12in (31cm); composition head; hand-painted facial features and hair; beige velveteen body; jointed arms and legs; swivel head; excelsior stuffing. *Courtesy Mimi Hiscox.*

Unmarked American "Eskimo Doll." Circa 1909. 16in (41cm); bisque doll head; brown glass eyes; long white silky mohair; Eskimo type outfit an integral part of body; beige felt hands and feet; jointed arms and legs; swivel head; excelsior stuffing. Doll produced in celebration of Peary and Cook's Arctic exposition (possibly made by the Strobel & Wilken Co.) [please refer to page 46, bottom right]). *Private collection.*

(Left) Georgene Product. "Uncle Wiggly." Circa 1943. 20in (51cm); cloth head and body; large black button eyes; hand-painted facial features; original clothes. (Center) Unidentified American manufacturer. Bear. Circa 1908. 10in (25cm); blonde colored mohair; shoe-button eyes; jointed arms and legs; swivel head; excelsior stuffing. (Right) Georgene Product. "Nurse Jane." Circa 1943. 20in (51cm); cloth head and body; large black button eyes; hand-painted facial features; original clothes. *Courtesy Mimi Hiscox.*

Above: A display of collectible sewing items are brought to life by adding teddy bears to the scene. A variety of unknown American manufactured bears from the early 1900s ranging in size from 10in (25cm) to 14in (36cm). *Photograph by Larry McDaniel.*

Left: Unidentified American manufacturer. Bears. Circa 1910. (Left) 21in (53cm). (Right) 25in (64cm); short gold mohair; glass eyes; jointed arms and legs; swivel heads; excelsior stuffing. Note unusual large head and round large snout. *Courtesy Rosemarie Binsteiner.*

Top Right: (Left) Unknown American manufacturer. Bear. Circa 1910; 17in (43cm); short gold bristle-type mohair; shoe-button eyes; jointed arms and legs; swivel head; excelsior stuffing. Appealing face and nice body lines. (Right) Volland. "Beloved Belinda." Circa 1920. 15in (38cm); cloth unjointed head and body; white button eyes; original clothes. *Courtesy Sherryl Shirran.*

Right: Unknown American manufacturers. Two bears (riding bear on wheels.) Circa 1910. 10in (25cm); golden mohair; shoe-button eyes; jointed arms and legs; swivel heads; excelsior stuffing. Bear on Wheels. Circa 1920. 18in (46cm) long golden colored mohair; glass eyes; unjointed legs; stationary head; metal spoked wheels. *Courtesy Audrey A. Meeneghen.*

Above left: Unknown American manufacturer. Bear. Circa 1915. 26in (66cm); silky white mohair; glass eyes; jointed arms and legs; swivel head; excelsior stuffing; pale tan pearl cotton stitched nose, mouth and claws. Unusual oversized head and large ears give bear a baby face appearance. *Courtesy Sherryl Shirran.*

Above right: (Left) Unknown American manufacturer. Bear. Circa 1915. 26in (66cm); short bristle-type gold mohair; glass eyes; jointed arms and legs; swivel head. Seated with the bear are two cloth unjointed "Buttercup" dolls with printed facial features and metal whisps of hair. Produced by the Modern Toy Co., Inc. Brooklyn, N.Y. *Courtesy Sherryl Shirran.*

Left: Unknown American Manufacturer. Bear. Circa 1910. 22in (56cm); cream-colored silky mohair; shoe-button eyes; jointed arms and legs; swivel head. *Courtesy Mort and Evelyn Wood.*

Above: Unknown American manufacturer. Bear. 1919. 20in (51cm); rich golden-cinnamon colored mohair; shoe-button eyes; excelsior stuffing. Purchased from original owner. *Courtesy Mort and Evelyn Wood.*

Above right: Unidentified American manufacturer. Bear. Circa 1915. 21in (53cm); short white mohair; glass eyes; tan stitched nose, mouth and claws; jointed arms and legs; swivel head. *Private collection.*

Right: Unidentified American manufacturer. Bear. Circa 1915. Approximate size 20in (51cm); white mohair; glass eyes; jointed arms and legs; swivel head; excelsior stuffing. Note large head, (flat at back, flat forehead), large round ears, square shaped snout and chunky torso compared to slender arms and legs. *Private collection.*

(Left) Unknown American manufacturer. Bear. Circa 1915. 23in (58cm); short gold bristle-type mohair; glass eyes; jointed arms and legs; swivel head. Large wide head, large round ears set toward the front of head and football shaped torso are definite distinguishing body traits to identify this bear as American. (Right) Schoenhut Sheep Toy 1910. 8in (20cm); wood; jointed; glass eyes. *Courtesy Barbara Lauver.*

Unknown American manufacturer. Bears. (Left) 1915. 18in (46cm); short, apricot-colored bristle-type mohair; glass eyes; fabric nose; ears sliced into head; jointed arms and legs; excelsior stuffing. (Right) 20in (51cm); gold bristle-type mohair; glass eyes; fabric nose; jointed arms and legs; swivel head; excelsior stuffing. Note: extra long narrow legs with almost no feet. Purchased from family of original owner. Family stated the bear was the sparring partner for his young owner whose dream was to be a boxer. His mother purported she repaired the poor bear hundreds of times. *Courtesy Joan Woessner. Photograph by Larry McDaniel.*

Unidentified American manufacturer. Bear. Circa 1920. 15in (38cm); white short bristle-type mohair head; red and royal blue short bristle-type mohair body; red mohair hat; glass eyes; black twisted cotton horizontally stitched nose; ears "sliced" into head; long narrow torso, arms and legs; small round feet; (arms and legs jointed with wires); swivel head; excelsior stuffing; torso seam closes at back. *Private collection. Photograph by Larry McDaniel.*

(Left) Unidentified American manufacturer. Bear. Circa 1915. 25in (64cm); bright gold short silky mohair; glass eyes; stitched (horizontal) brown twisted pearl cotton nose and mouth; jointed arms and legs; swivel head; excelsior stuffing. (Right) Unidentified American manufacturer. Bear. Circa 1915. 25in (64cm); bright gold short silky mohair; stitched (horizontal) brown twisted pearl cotton nose and mouth; jointed arms and legs; swivel head; excelsior stuffing. Slender straight arms and legs with small feet, football shaped torsos, round head and the bright gold mohair are all typical of domestically made bears from 1915 to the 1920s. *Courtesy Martha and Jim Hession.*

Two typical American bears (left 22in [56cm] right 17in [43cm]) from around the 1920s. Short bristle-type mohair in bright orangy-gold, glass stick pin eyes; ears "sliced" into round shaped heads, long narrow torsos, straight, narrow arms and legs; small feet; small stitched (horizontal) black cotton nose, mouth and claws; body stuffed firm with excelsior. *Courtesy Martha and Jim Hession.*

Unidentified American manufacturer. Bear. Circa 1920. 19in (48cm); short silky brown mohair; glass eyes; jointed arms and legs; swivel head; excelsior stuffing (firmly stuffed). Straight narrow torso, arms and legs. *Courtesy Nelson Davis.*

Above: Unidentified American manufacturer. Circa 1920. 26in (66cm); bright gold silky mohair; glass eyes; excelsior stuffing. Bright gold mohair was used on a large percentage of American bears during the 1920s. *Courtesy Mort and Evelyn Wood.*

Right: "Long-Voice" bear. Circa 1914. 12in (31cm); gold mohair; glass eyes; jointed arms; swivel head; excelsior stuffed head. Long-voice is encased in body. When released after being pressed down, emits a long-drawn-out squeal, which makes it the item for Halloween (stated in their 1914 advertisement in *Playthings* magazine). *Private collection.*

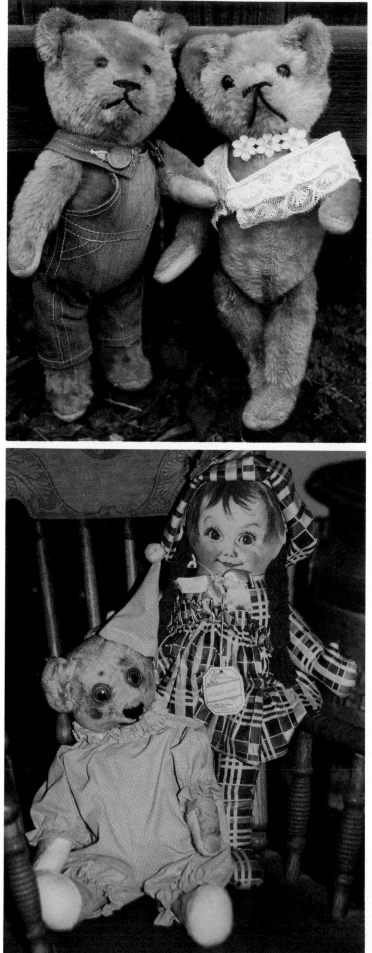

Above left: Unknown American manufacturer. Bears. Circa 1920. 12in (31cm); (left) short bristle-type gold mohair; glass eyes. (Right) short bristle-type pale gold mohair; shoe-button eyes. Both bears are fully jointed and stuffed with excelsior. Note: typical American football-shaped body with non-defined arms and legs with vestigial feet distinctly different to the shape of their head. *Courtesy Susie Carlson.*

Above right: Clown bears and dolls have always been a fun and desirable addition to doll and bear collections. These American versions are quite unusual. (Front) Bear. Circa 1930. 12in (31cm); pink, blue and white mohair; glass eyes; jointed arms and legs; swivel head; excelsior stuffing. (Back right) Bear. Circa 1920. 13in (33cm); beige fabric head feet and paw pads; red and blue felt outfit (an integral part of body); blue felt hat; shoe-button eyes; swivel head; "sliced-in" ears; jointed arms; stationary legs. (Back left) Clown Doll. Circa 1930. 11in (28cm); composition hand-painted head and hands; cloth jointed body; original clothes. *Courtesy Sherryl Shirran.*

Left: (Left) Unidentified American manufacturer. "Sleep Eyed" bear. Circa 1924. 15in (38cm); rust-colored mohair (worn); sleep celluloid eyes; jointed arms and legs; swivel head; excelsior stuffing. (Right) Georgene Novelty. "Peggy Ann." Circa 1930. Unjointed cloth head and body; printed facial features; rust-colored yarn pigtails; checkered fabric clothes an integral part of body. Front of original hang tag reads: "Art in Cloth Dolls Peggy Ann", reverse of tag reads: "An original Georgene Novelty/Copy Maude Tousley Fangel." *Courtesy Mimi Hiscox.*

Right: (Left) Unidentified American manufacturer. Bear with Movable Eyes. Circa 1924. 14in (36cm); long silky gold mohair; celluloid movable googlie-type eyes; jointed arms and legs; swivel head. (Center) National French and Novelty Co. Bear with Moveable Eyes. Circa 1924. 14in (36cm); dark honey-colored mohair; sleeping celluloid eyes (eyes close like a sleeping doll when in horizontal position); jointed arms and legs; swivel head; excelsior stuffing. (Right) National French Novelty Co. Sleeping Toodles Dog. Circa 1924. 10in (25cm) long by 8in (20cm) high. White and gold mohair; sleeping celluloid eyes; unjointed legs; swivel head. Annette Himstedt doll. 1989. *Photograph by Larry McDaniel.*

Below left: Your bears can enhance the decor of your home. Unknown American manufacturer. Bear. Circa 1930. Pale gold mohair; glass eyes; jointed arms and legs; swivel head. Dressed in a long white Victorian christening dress. Doll. Antique reproduction of a baby Bru by American doll artist Gordona Little. 12in (31cm). *Courtesy Joan Woessner. Photograph by Larry McDaniel.*

Below right: This rare 1930 American (manufacturer unknown) musical (squeeze type music box concealed in torso) bear (back) doesn't quite know where to start the restoration process of the small 1910 extremely "well loved" American bear (front). *Photograph by Larry McDaniel.*

Left: Unidentified American manufacturer. Bears With Movable Eyes. Circa 1930. (Back) honey-colored mohair. (Front) blonde mohair. Celluloid sleep eyes; jointed arms and legs; swivel head; excelsior stuffing. Elongated snout and feet on bear in front give bear lots of character. *Courtesy Sherryl Shirran.*

Right: Unknown American manufacturer. Bears. (Left) Circa 1920. 16in (41cm); dark rust-colored rayon and cotton plush; glass eyes; jointed arms and legs; swivel head; excelsior stuffing. Body traits reflect American design; football shaped body; arms are straight and the shapeless legs have extremely small feet, fairly large round head. (Right) Circa 1940. Deep rust-colored shaggy rayon and cotton plush; flat copper-colored movable plastic disk eyes; velveteen paw pads; soft stuffing. Note large head and chunky body. *Courtesy Susie Carlson.*

Right: Unknown American manufacturer. Bear. Circa 1930. 12in (31cm); bright cinnamon, long luxuriant mohair; shaved snout; amber glass eyes; jointed arms and legs; swivel head; kapok stuffed body; excelsior stuffed head. The long rich cinnamon-colored mohair is of a color much favored by American manufacturers during the 1930s and 1940s. *Courtesy Susie Carlson.*

Left: Pat Todd began collecting vinyl faced bears when you could purchase them for under $20. Today these appealing characters produced around 1950-1960 have become harder to find and considerably more expensive than Pat's early collecting days. Various American manufacturers designs are pictured. Note: full vinyl faces, vinyl snouts, plastic eyes, painted eyes and movable eyes are pictured. The majority of these 1950s and 1960s bears are unjointed and produced in rayon plush. *Courtesy Pat Todd.*

59

Chapter Three

American Teddy Bear Manufacturers

Ideal Toy Company

Even though there has been much controversy about the role of the Ideal Toy Company in the birth of the teddy bear, there is no doubt that the New York Stock Exchange-listed firm is greatly responsible for the popularity of teddy bears both in this country and abroad.

Legend has it that in 1902, when Morris Mitchom (Ideal's founder) saw the now-famous Clifford Berryman cartoon of President Roosevelt's encounter with a bear, he was inspired. His wife stitched a lovable, jointed bear by hand and the couple displayed their creation in the window of their small store in Brooklyn, NY.

They say that Mitchom then wrote to Teddy Roosevelt to elicit his permission to name the animal "Teddy." And the president acquiesced.

This legendary beginning has never been completely documented, but most accept (at least parts of it) as true.

When the Butler Brothers, a large wholesaler who knew a sure thing when they saw one, bought all of the already made bears the Mitchoms had, the idea took off like wildfire. Butler backed Mitchoms' credit with plush producing mills and the Ideal Novelty Toy Company was born. (In 1938, the name was shortened to the Ideal Toy Company.)

Ideal Bears. 1907. (Left 19in [48cm] right 13in [33cm]) short gold bristle-type mohair; shoe-button eyes; black twisted pearl cotton vertically stitched nose; jointed arms and legs; swivel head; excelsior stuffing; torso seam closed in front. Characteristics of Ideal: triangle shaped head; large round ears; long narrow torso; arms set low; foot pads come to a point.

Ideal Bear. Circa 1907. 12in (31cm); gold mohair; shoe-button eyes; black fabric nose; jointed arms and legs; swivel head; excelsior stuffing. Nose is slightly turned up; hump on back is high; head positioned slightly forward on torso. *Private collection.*

Ideal Bear. Circa 1907. 18in (46cm); pale gold mohair shoe-button eyes; jointed arms and legs; swivel head; excelsior stuffing. Rare early design. *Courtesy Barbara Baldwin.*

The firm really solidified in 1907 after it moved to Brooklyn and produced its first American character doll (a boy doll called "The Yellow Kid"). In 1912, Abraham Katz joined the company. He grew to play a major role in its success. Morris Mitchom's son, Benjamin, grew to be a great marketer within the toy industry.

Over the years, Ideals' production plant grew and grew to more than 600,000 square feet in Hollis (New Jersey) and a headquarters of a million square feet in the Newark Meadowlands.

Among the famous toys produced by Ideal are Shirley Temple, Sparkle Plenty, Patty Playpal, Robert the Talking Robot and Evel Knieval. In the early 1950s, Ideal was authorized to create Smokey Bear (see page 120).

Even though no definitive identification has been associated with bears manufactured by this renowned company in the early years, it is my experience that the main characteristics to look for are a wide triangular head, large widely set ears, arms positioned low on shoulders, pads on the feet coming to a point, short mohair and fairly long and slender bodies.

IDEAL®

1903 - 1986

Ideal, Inc.

A Subsidiary of
VIEW-MASTER IDEAL
GROUP, INC.

Many of the most familiar bears to collectors were those owned during their own childhood. The decade of the fifties was a very productive period for Ideal and many different designs with the original Ideal tag have been discovered by collectors. A feature considerably used on these cute bears were faces molded in vinyl with painted features. Many had adorable big sleep eyes. The eyes were made of plastic with tin eyelids and bristle eyelashes. The majority were unjointed with chunky soft bodies made in beautiful colors of rayon plush.

In 1983, CBS bought Ideal for $58 million. View-Master (makers of the 3-D viewers) purchased Ideal and finally the toy company was made part of Tyco Toys, Inc. Now, Ideal is an indirect wholly-owned subsidiary of Tyco Toys.

Ideal began as a mom and pop operation sewing teddy bears in their store. Over the years it grew to a large conglomerate. But Ideal has never compromised the fun and quality toys produced for several generations of America's children.

The image of Ideal's Smithsonian bear (for further information on the Smithsonian Bear please refer to page 63, top right) is superimposed into Clifford Berryman's famous cartoon (for further information on Berryman's cartoon please refer to page 10, bottom left) for the cover of Ideal's 1986 catalog. It is Berryman's famous cartoon that the Ideal Novelty & Toy Company reports inspired Morris Mitchom (founder of the company) to create his first teddy bear. *Courtesy Gerald Freeman Inc.*

Ideal Bear. Circa 1909. 25in (64cm); short, blonde, bristle-type mohair; glass eyes; jointed arms and legs; thin, pinkish beige felt pads; swivel head; excelsior stuffing. Note American characteristics: round head (flat on back); large round ears; black twisted pearl cotton nose (horizontally stitched), mouth and claws; long curved rather narrow arms; large feet, pronounced hump on back, long oval torso, body shaped around large tilt-type growler (5in [13cm] long by 3in [8cm] in diameter); body seam closed in front. Bear was found in 1994 in a trunk in the loft of an old barn in Vista, California. *Courtesy Martha and Jim Hession.*

Right: Benjamin Mitchom, son of Morris Mitchom founder of the Ideal Novelty & Toy Company presented this early 1900s Ideal Bear to President Theodore Roosevelt's grandson, Kermit, and his family (1963). The Roosevelts decided the teddy bear named for the President should be donated to the Smithsonian Institute. *Courtesy Smithsonian Institute.*

Below left: Barbara Baldwin's young daughter Jessica models Barbara's rare acquisition - an early 1900s Ideal teddy bear muff. *Courtesy Barbara Baldwin.*

Below right: Ideal. Bear. Circa 1920. 18in (46cm); gold mohair; glass eyes; jointed arms and legs; excelsior stuffing. *Courtesy Barbara Baldwin.*

Left: Ideal. Bear. Circa 1910. 22in (56cm); rich cinnamon-colored mohair; shoe-button eyes; black fabric nose; jointed arms and legs; swivel head; excelsior stuffing. Facial features, fabric nose, side placement of ears, deeply set eyes are all characteristics of early bears produced by the Ideal Toy Company. *Courtesy Mort and Evelyn Wood.*

Below: (Left to right) Ideal. Bear. Circa 1950. 13in (33cm); bright cinnamon-colored rayon plush; white rayon plush paw pads and inner ears; vinyl snout with hand-painted features; plastic eyes; unjointed arms and legs; stationary head. Label sewn into side seam reads: "Ideal Toy Company." Ideal. Bear. 1978. "Collectors Edition." 16in (41cm); caramel colored acrylic plush; short pale caramel-colored acrylic plush inset snout; plastic eyes; unjointed arms and legs; stationary head. Ideal. Bear. Circa 1939. 12in (31cm); rich cinnamon-colored mohair; glass eyes; jointed arms and legs; swivel head; hard resin nose; excelsior stuffed head; kapok stuffed body; cardboard tag attached to bear reads: "An Ideal Ultrafine Animal/Ideal Novelty and Toy Co." To my knowledge, no pre-1930 Ideal teddy bear has yet been found with its original tag.

Gund

Perhaps the most outstanding feature of this upscale, century-old toy company is that it is still run by descendants of its earliest employee.

Founded by Adolph Gund in 1898 in Norwalk, Connecticut, the company manufactured belts, necklaces, novelties and handmade stuffed toys. Never realizing the legacy he would leave to the toy world, Adolph Gund, in response to a customer request, jumped on the teddy bear wagon in 1906. He himself bought a few yards of plush, took the materials home with him and burned the midnight oil to make four different sizes of teddy bears ranging from 10in (25cm) to 16in (41cm) tall. The next year he followed quickly with Easter rabbits and even a possum. By 1910, Gund was incorporated and ready to introduce its first complete line of stuffed toys.

Around 1915, a young man by the name of Jacob (Jack) Swedlin joined the company. He took a menial job with Gund to help support his emigrant Russian family where he was the oldest of seven children. Three years later he was head of the Cutting Department, and later was promoted to the position of personal assistant to Adolph Gund.

By that time, Gund was consistently producing four sizes of bears, ranging from 10in to 16in (25cm to 41cm).

The original corporation dissolved in 1925. The assets were taken over by Jacob Swedlin, who, according to his boss, was "really the only one who (had) the courage and foresight to continue the business." His two brothers joined him in the new organization. His brother Abraham (Abe) served as executive vice president and treasurer and Louis (L.) was sales manager. (page 67, bottom right). Gund has been in the Swedlin family ever since.

The founder's predictions proved true. Swedlin changed a number of manufacturing methods. One of the most important early ones was a die-cutting process using a mallet and a shaped piece of metal against pieces of cloth. This limited the number of cloth layers which could be cut, and if the operators were sloppy, pieces turned out irregular. Swedlin developed the first use of a clicking machine which cut many more layers at a time with more accuracy.

Perhaps the most radical changes, though, were in the field of foam rubber and synthetic foam products. According to a 1964 interview in the July issue of *Playthings*, Mr. J. "Jack" Swedlin felt "synthetics work just as well in some instances as long as they don't deteriorate or exude unpleasant odors."

Gund is also attributed with producing the first affordable mass-produced musical toys for just $3.98. That was in 1949, the year in which "Nancy Lou," a percale cotton-stuffed doll with a composition mask face and yarn curls was marketed for just under $3.00.

Another first for Gund was the combination of a molded vinyl face with a fabric body. "Regal Beagle" and "Boopsie Bear" popularized the method in 1952. Gund also updated the fabric rider animals which were on wheels earlier on, and put them on rockers instead.

In the early '70s, Gund's huggable "Luv-Me-Bear" made toy industry history by introducing the now-famous technique of understuffing each animal and using softer materials.

Identification may prove somewhat difficult since prior to 1940 there were no laws requiring sewn in labels, so collectors must rely on the preservation of hangtags with product information. Early Gund tags read: "A Gund Product, A Toy of Quality and Distinction." From World War Two on, the tags show the stylized "G" most often appearing as a rabbit with ears and whiskers. From the mid-1960s, until 1987 straight block type featured a signature bear's head above the letter "U"; and from 1987 the current capital book type "GUND" has been the official logo.

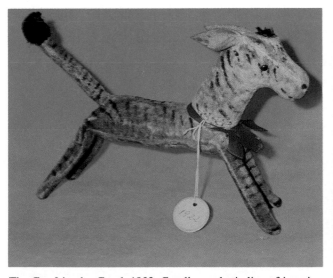

The Gee Line by Gund. 1922. Gund's acrobatic line of jumping animals. Patented and exclusive to Gund. Made in six characters: Giraffe, Tiger, Horse, Dog, Cat and Monkey. Made of colored velveteen. By pressing down hind legs, then suddenly releasing, the animal will do a complete somersault. *Courtesy Gund.*

Velveteen was used by Gund for many of their animals during the 1920s. *Courtesy Gund.*

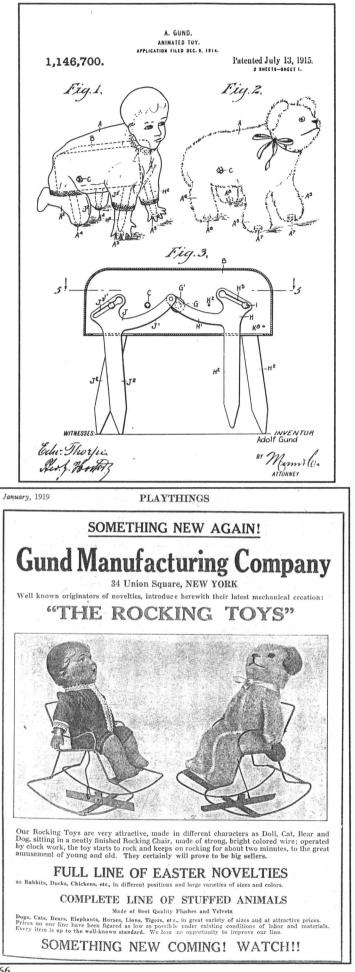

Top left: A. Gund filed the application for this animated toy December 9, 1914. This animated A. Gund creation was advertised in *Playthings* magazine in their January 1915 issue (please see caption below). *Courtesy Gund.*

Top right: Gund Manufacturing Company advertised their new animated invention "Creeping Baby" and "Walking Animals" in the January 1915 issue of *Playthings* magazine. Courtesy Playthings.

Left: Gund Manufacturing Company produced these fun "Rocking Toys" in 1919. A doll, bear, cat, and a dog were made sitting in strong, bright colored wire chairs operated by clock work. *Courtesy* Playthings.

Sometimes identification may be aided by checking the address on the label. If the label shows a New York City address, the bear was made between 1940 and 1956.

The company's factory moved to Brooklyn in 1956. Gund's showroom is the oldest tenant (dating back to the '20s) at 200 Fifth Avenue Toy Center in New York City. However, its factory and offices moved to New Jersey in 1973 and in 1988 moved to even more extensive facilities in Edison.

In the fall of 1992, Gund, Inc. announced the formation of two new subsidiaries to serve the European Community. America's oldest soft toy company now will warehouse their inventory in Europe to supply customers abroad on an "as needed" basis.

To this day, Gund, Inc., continues as a privately-held corporation with Bruce Raiffe as president, Rita Raiffe (Swedlin's daughter) as director of design, supervising all designs, color and quality and Herbert Raiffe serving as chairman. Shari Meltzer, who is no relation to any of the Raiffe family, has been at Gund since 1981 and is now marketing manager.

Three fairly distinct categories now comprise the Gund offerings. There is the standard, "made-to-be-loved" Gund line; a slightly more expensive, collectible assortment and the TOBY® and Golden Teddy award-winning Signature Collection, which is a high-end grouping available in limited and numbered editions.

The company is well-known for their association with cartoon characters beginning with the velveteen *Felix the Cat* in 1925. Acrobatic animals which tumbled when squeezed were also popular during this era. In the '40s and '50s, floppy sleepy animals called Dreamies (page 71) were introduced as well as a "Regal" line of plush pets with molded faces and moving eyes.

MECHANICAL CHARACTERS

No. 5926

Dancing Duck. A quaint number done in velvet with wings of three contrasting colors. Stands 10½ inches.

This line of mechanical dancing animals is one of the BEST and most POPULAR ON THE MARKET TODAY. Every number is attractive, flashily dressed and WELL made. A feature display will sell a great many of these dancers. Attention is called to "Felix the Cat," that famous movie cartoon character. Each dancer packed in an individual, attractively lithographed box.

No. 2923

Dancing Felix the Cat. Pat Sullivan's famous movie character. Measures 10½". Dressed in Velvet. Has glass eyes, glass nose and felt ears.

No. 2928

Dancing Bluebird. A happy number backed in blue velvet and breasted in red velvet with tri-colored wings measuring 10½"

No. 2933

Dancing Bell Hop Monkey. Dressed in red imitation jacket, and black trousers, has buttons on breast and wears a red cap.

A variety of mechanical dancing animals were produced by Gund during the 1920s. *Courtesy Gund.*

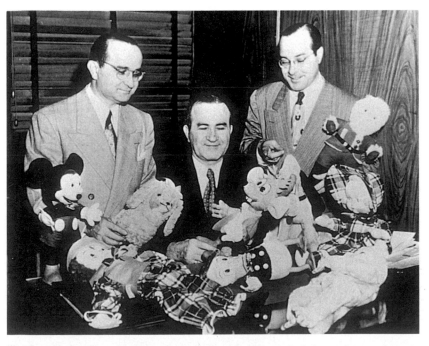

The Swedlin brothers: Abraham, (center), Jacob and Louis L. John, took an active role in their toy industry and in their community. Gund was one of the 50 manufacturers that organized the Stuffed Toy Manufacturers Association, and served as its president in 1937. *Courtesy Gund.*

(Left) Gund Dog. Circa 1927. Printed striped silk velvet; glass eyes; unjointed; excelsior stuffing. (Right) Gund. *Felix the Cat.* Circa 1930. *Felix* (copyright Pat Sullivan) was introduced into the Gund line in 1927. Featured for many years in Gund's catalogs, they produced this intriguing famous movie cartoon character with many variations including a mechanical dancing version made in black velvet. *Courtesy Gund.*

Gund first introduced Easter rabbits to their line in 1907. Appealingly dressed in colorful costumes, the interest in this popular animal has been fairly consistent throughout Gund's history. Pictured are examples of four Gund rabbits highly sought after by collectors today. *Cowboy Peter Rabbit* (top left) was produced in 1937 and *Molly* and *Peter Rabbit* was produced in 1939 and 1940. *Courtesy Gund.*

(Left) Gund *Dreamie Cat* 1941. Fuzzy white plush; *Dreamie* mask face with painted features; pink velvet lined ears. Special construction enables cat to assume many cuddly positions. Due to the popularity of this design, several other adorable fluffy animals with pressed mask faces and dreamie eyes were produced in the *Dreamie* series including a rabbit bear and panda. (Right) *Bonny Scotsman* Bunny. 1937. *Mary Lou* Tyrolean girl Bunny. 1938. The cute pressed doll faces with painted features were used on many of Gund's rabbit designs. *Courtesy Gund.*

Other cartoon characters developed by Gund include Mickey and Minnie Mouse (page 70, top and page 69, top), Donald Duck (page 69, middle), and Pluto. Collectors know that a long list of Gund produced Disney characters includes: Snow White and the Seven Dwarfs, Cinderella, Jungle Book animals, Mary Poppins, Lady and the Tramp, Dumbo, Goofy and the Shaggy Dog.

From the mid 1930s to 1969, Gund was the official Disney® licensee. At that time, Disney® took most of its licensed characters in-house. However, Gund continued to produce Winnie-the-Pooh. The link-up of Disney®'s Winnie-the-Pooh and Gund goes back to the 1960s when the classic A.A. Milne stories became Disney® animated features. Toward the end of that decade, Gund made a plush Winnie-the-Pooh and also a vinyl doll of Christopher Robin. Both were marketed through Sears, Roebuck and Company from 1970 to 1993. Now Gund is also the licensee for Classic Winnie-the-Pooh (page 78) and friends, based on the Milne stories and the drawings originally done by E.H. Shepard.

The Disney® connection doesn't end here. Gund was one of the original participants in Disney®'s annual Teddy Bear convention, and produced Mickey's Teddy based on Disney®'s

Top right: (Left) Gund *Minnie Mouse*. 1930. 13in (33cm); short black rayon plush; fabric mask face; painted facial features; white felt hands; black felt ears; black felt tail; unjointed arms and legs; stationary head; dressed in a red, white spotted skirt; red satin bows at ears; red painted oilcloth, high-heeled shoes. Label reads: "Gund Mfg. Co. (J. Swedlin Inc.)" Reverse: "Minnie Mouse/copyright, Walt Disney Productions." (Right) Gund. *Donald Duck*. 1950. 9in (23cm); painted vinyl face; rayon plush unjointed body; felt paws and feet; chiming musical ball encased in body. Label reads: "Gund Mfg. Co/J.Swedlin Inc." Reverse: "Donald Duck/Walt Disney Productions." *Photograph by Larry McDaniel.*

Center right: Gund *Donald Duck* (12in [31cm]), *Huey*, *Dewey* and *Louie* (9in [23cm]); 1930. Rayon silk plush bodies; yellow felt beaks and feet. White felt hands; celluloid eyes, (*Donald Duck* has painted eyes); unjointed arms and legs; stationary head. Gund identification label sewn into the side seam of each duck. *Photograph by Larry McDaniel.*

Bottom right: (Left) Gund *Bongo*. 1949. 13in (33cm); rich brown rayon plush; fabric mask face; painted facial features; unjointed body; stationary head. Label reads: "Gund Mfg. Co/J. Swedlin Inc." Reverse: "Bongo/copyright Walt Disney." (Right) Gund *Lulu-Belle*. 1949. 13in (33cm); pale gold rayon plush; fabric mask face; painted facial features; unjointed body; stationary head. Label reads: "Gund Mfg. Co/J. Swedlin Inc." Reverse "Bongo/copyright Walt Disney." *Bongo* and *Lulu* were produced by Gund from 1949 to 1952. Vinyl-faced version of these appealing Disney® characters were made by Gund in 1957 (one year only). *Photograph by Larry McDaniel.*

Left: *Mickey Mouse* the favorite of all Disney® characters was produced by Gund from 1947 to 1969. This wonderful large-size (approximate size 28in [71cm]) is unjointed with floppy legs, short pile rayon plush, white mask painted face; black felt ears; white felt hands; red trousers. He has a red ribbon around his neck. *Courtesy Gund.*

Below: These beautiful silky mohair, fully-jointed teddy bears were made by Gund during the 1930s. *Courtesy Gund.*

logo for the event. The company is also responsible for the popular Disney® babies, sold only at Disney® theme parks.

In 1979, Gund introduced "Collector Classics," which continues to be an important part of their product line. This grouping began with a family of six huggable bears from 6in to 4ft (15cm - 112cm). Honey Bear is one outstanding bear from that debut series. Other bears in the grouping are Bearpersons: Waldo, Chester, Barney, Vanilla and Chocolate Truffles.

The most popular animal Gund ever made was Snuffles, a little bear with an upturned face who begs to be played with. He comes in pink, tan, white and brown. After 13 years, Snuffles holds on to his "star quality" and still remains a perennial favorite for Gund.

In 1982, Bialosky Bear was introduced by the company. A reproduction of the 1907 antique bear is featured each year on the cover of the "Teddy Bear Calendar" (Workman Publishing). The first edition was dressed in a tuxedo, sailor suit or in golfing attire and was available in three sizes. Later editions included a skier, artist, pilot, camper, Pierrot, Santa and a team player. A few Gloryosky Bialoskys were also made by Gund, as well as a white Suzie bear.

The release of new bears is engineered carefully. One notable example is the Gundy Bear, first commemorating Gund's 85th birthday in 1983. By 1987, this bear had evolved to a wooly brown bear with velveteen paw pads (9in [23cm]). He came in a special gift box...another success in Gund's leading edge formula. Gundy grows in popularity year after year.

Gund also is on the forefront with collectibles. Now Gund still continues its award-winning Signature Collection, a special series of the finest handmade, limited edition, American-style bears. These bears have longer plush, often with leather

Illustration 150. Gund Bear. Circa 1930. Cinnamon-colored curly plush; amber-colored eyes; jointed arms and legs; swivel head. Courtesy Gund.

Illustration 151. Gund Bear. Circa 1930. Cinnamon-colored curly plush; inset light brown fabric snout; clamped-in eyes; jointed arms and legs; swivel head. Note paw pads applied by stitching on the right side of the fabric. Courtesy Gund.

or suede pads and are intended for adult collectors. These bears are fully articulated and are trimmed with distinctive ribbons and special edition tag. Each bear is signed and numbered by Rita Swedlin Raiffe in editions of 400-800 pieces.

About distributed by Gund are The Canterbury Bears, fine handcrafted English bears which have a loyal following among teddy bear collectors the world over. (Page 76.)

About 250-300 new Gund creations are introduced at the February Toy Fair held in New York. The company then debuts new additions again mid-year. One such addition to join the Gund family are the Cinnabears, a wonderful new addition of a sweetly-designed, spicy-scented family of country bears. Each has his or her own legend, intricately woven into a visually romantic tale. (Page 80 and page 81, top.)

Gund's newest release of the Cinnabear bears combines beautifully appealing creations with a rich, interwoven tapestry of family history — all wrapped up in the ever-nurturing fragrance of spicy cinnamon and cloves.

The bear artist whose creativity and talent gave birth to Cinnabear is Gisele Nash. Gisele, mother of three, is an especially gifted artist whose work has won her countless awards and notoriety. Throughout her young life, Gisele's prodigious talents have surfaced in many areas from set design to ceramic sculpture.

Gund. Clown *Monkigund*. 1949. Colorful unjointed novelty clown monkeys with short pile plush were produced by Gund with the painted face mask. The face mask design patent was filed by Gund August 1, 1942. *Courtesy Gund.*

F.W. Woolnough Corp. (Left) *Cuddle Bear and Baby*. Circa 1940. Advertised in their catalog their toys were "Made of delustered rayon plush, in a soft cuddle type pattern that is huggable and loveable. Has hand embroidered nose and mouth." (Right) F.W. Woolnough Corp Dog. Circa 1940. F.W. Woolnough was a division of Gund. Courtesy Gund.

Above left: These colorful silk plush unjointed rabbits with velvet lined ears and pink eyes were produced by Gund during the 1940s. *Courtesy Gund.*

Above right: Gund standing Balloon Panda with Tuxedo Tails. Circa 1938. White silk plush head, paws and feet; inset white vinyl snout with hand-painted features; clamped-in movable eyes; unjointed body; red silk plush tuxedo jacket and blue silk plush "balloon" shaped pants are an integral part of body. *Courtesy Gund.*

Right: Gund. *Cuddle* Pandas. Circa 1939. Unjointed bodies; black and white plush; clamped-in moving eyes (with the exception of the glass-eyed versions pictured bottom left and top right); soft stuffing. Note plastic and embroidered noses were used. Two Pandas right of the picture were called *Four Circle Cuddle Pandas* because of the contrasting color on the four circle hands and feet. Gund's pandas were originally produced with collars or ribbon with a jingle bell on the neck. *Courtesy Gund.*

Gund is very proud of the family values emulated in the characters and the delightful stories surrounding the Cinnabear family.

The Cinnabear Family Tree includes the likes of Nutmeg O'Bear (Nana Nutmeg, matriarch and chronicler of family history); Grandpa Basil, a skilled woodmaker; their son Herb, an entrepreneur married to Clove R. Laurel; their children Dill, Rosemary and Parsley; and Uncle Salty. Each stands alone and as part of the whole with a host of warm, loving stories and adventures.

Gund plans to accessorize the line with additional outfits and furnishings. Possible projected plans call for newsletters and a club.

Another example of Gund's creativity in the collectible marketplace is The Littlest Bears series. Until now, miniature bears have proven too costly to mass market. However, Gund's new line features an entire family of miniature bears, complete with furniture and accessories. The handmade bears are all fully jointed and come in a package which contains an original, hand-painted background scene. Nancy

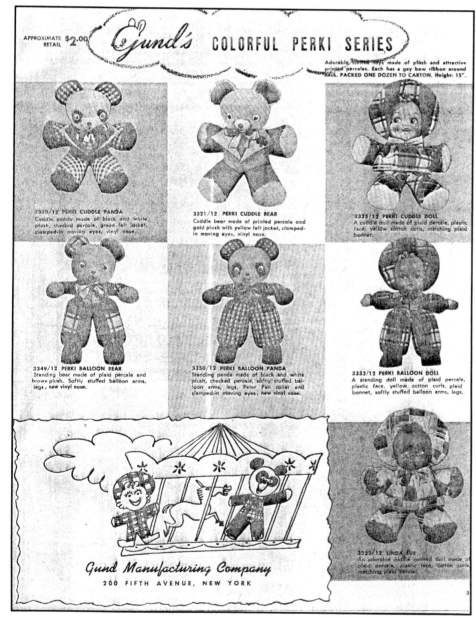

Top left: (Left) Gund. *Perki Balloon Panda*. Circa 1942. White plush head; black and white fabric outfit an integral part of body; moving clamped-in eyes; unjointed standing body; stationary head; soft stuffing (please see bottom illustration for example of *Perki Balloon Panda* pictured in Gund's 1942 catalog). (Right) Gund Panda. Circa 1940. Black and white plush; moving clamped-in eyes; unjointed standing body; stationary head; soft stuffing. *Courtesy Gund.*

Bottom left: Gund's *Colorful Perki Series*. In 1942 Gund advertised animals and dolls with percale bodies; shaggy plush heads and paw and foot pads and dolls with plaid percale bodies and bonnets and molded hand painted faces. *Courtesy Gund.*

Above left: Gund. *Teddi Gund.* Circa 1948; 16in (41cm); gold mohair; inset short pile mohair snout; glass eyes; jointed arms and legs; swivel head; kapok stuffing. Note: large head; large slightly cupped ears; shield shaped nose; stitched mouth forms smile; thin, felt paw pads, exterior stitching (visible) applied paw pads and inset snout. Remains of manufacturer's label stitched into right arm seam. *Photograph by Larry McDaniel.*

Above right: Gund. *Cubbie Gund.* Bear. Circa 1952. 10in (25cm); brown rayon plush; cream-colored rayon plush paw pads and inside ears; painted features on molded vinyl snout; white plastic eyes with black plastic movable disk under clear plastic covering; unjointed arms and legs; stationary head; soft stuffing. Manufacturers label sewn into right side seam. *Photograph by Larry McDaniel.*

Right: Gund's 1950s catalog advertised *Boopsy Bears* with cheerful molded vinyl faces, hand-painted facial features and a delightful "growler voice." *Boopsy and Babe* were an irresistible combination of a lovable Mama Bear and her darling Baby Bear. *Courtesy Gund.*

Left: The most popular character of Gund's 1950s line was *Regal Beagle* and the Regal line of plush toys with molded vinyl faces and sleep eyes. *Courtesy Gund.*

Below left: When my niece Carly Parris (right), visited me from England in 1993 I asked her and my granddaughter Frances Tipton (left) to select some of my Gund bears to pose with. Frances chose Gund's *Sweet Thing*. This vibrant violet-colored mohair bear was produced in an edition of 500 in 1993. Carly chose Canterbury Bears' *Rufus*. (distributed by Gund.) This wonderful red German mohair bear sports a green satin ribbon with a black feather set in a mount. Limited edition to 500. *Courtesy Gund.*

Below right: I cannot help but boast that this photogenic pair are two of my all-time favorites: my niece Carly Parris and her bear, Gund's 1993 creation *Gold Dust* (Limited edition 650.)

Villasenor-Cordaro, who has been involved with the teddy bear and doll world for many years conceived the tiny critters. They are intended for both children and adults. The 20 items in the line are designed for existing collectors, as well as those who couldn't afford smaller bears before.

Since Gund was established in 1898, some of the original antique Gund pieces have sold for prices as high as $2000 in the collector's market.

Gund's collective imaginations are formidable, giving life to up to 500 products in a year, with new designs constantly appearing. They seem to have a universal appeal, capturing hearts and imaginations of young and old alike.

Someday Gund may have its own collectible museum. Jacob Swedlin and his daughter Rita kept samples of much of everything manufactured by the company from the very beginning. With well-kept examples of initial designs to finished product, catalog photos, registered patents, advertisements and patterns, the majority of the collection was left to Rita Raiffe by her father. It encompasses the years 1912 through today and she continues to add to the collection at every opportunity. She hopes that the collection will be a tribute to her father and the company of Gund, as well as a legacy to her sons, grandchildren and to collectors everywhere.

Right: F. W. Woolnough (A division of Gund) advertised *Winnie-the-Pooh* in *Playthings* 1930 magazine. This bright, golden mohair bear with pot belly and short chunky legs was an appealing rendition of A. A. Milne's famous literary character *Winnie-the-Pooh*. (Please refer to photo shown below for plush example of F. W. Woolnough's Winnie-the-Pooh.) *Courtesy* Playthings.

Well, Well, Well!

Look Who's Here!

Don't say Teddy Bear—
Say "Winnie-The-Pooh"

YESSIR—*it's*

WINNIE-THE-POOH

And

He's Picked Out WOOLNOUGH

to make him into Perfect Toy Form for the thousands and thousands of kiddies who have read about him in A. A. Milne's famous Juvenile Books (over 1,000,000 sold in America alone).

Ladies and Gentlemen, make no mistake about it—WINNIE THE POOH will be *the* Toy Feature of the season. Not only is he the most lovable children's character of all times, but he's by all odds the most distinctive and best looking pet you ever saw.

Freshen up your Animal Display with this exclusive Woolnough Creation. Show WINNIE THE POOH in your toy department and see how many friends he has who will want to buy him right away. Give your advertising and publicity department the opportunity they have long desired and watch them both eagerly feature WINNIE-THE-POOH.

Write for Samples.

F. W. WOOLNOUGH CO., Inc.

45 EAST 17th STREET, NEW YORK

We will appreciate your courtesy in mentioning PLAYTHINGS

Right: (Back) F. W. Woolnough Co. *Winnie-the-Pooh*. Circa 1930. 14in (36cm); gold mohair; button eyes (possibly replaced); jointed arms and legs; swivel head. (Front left to right) Gund. *Winnie-the-Pooh*. Circa 1960. 7in (18cm); bright gold velveteen; black felt eyes, nose and eye brows; unjointed body; stationary head; wood chips stuffing; red knit sweater. Gund. *Winnie-the-Pooh*. Circa 1960. 10in (25cm); gold plush; unjointed arms and legs (legs sewn in seated position); stationary head; glass eyes; knitted sweater with matching cap. F. W. Woolnough Co., *Winnie-the-Pooh*. Circa 1930. 9in (23cm); bright gold mohair; fully jointed; glass eyes (replaced). (Please refer to photo shown above for F. W. Woolnough Co., advertisement for *Winnie-the-Pooh*.) Please note F. W. Woolnough Co. was a division of Gund.

Left: The beautiful decorated shadow box scenes tell a story for each of the *Littlest Bears* by Gund (please refer to the illustration below for information regarding the *Littlest Bears*). *Courtesy Gund.*

Below: The *Littlest Bears* by Gund. 1994. These exquisite miniature works of art are all handmade of fine materials and are fully-jointed, poseable, dressed and accessorized to compliment their own beautiful setting (please refer to the illustration above for example of setting). The *Littlest Bears* project is the brainchild of Nancy Villasenor-Cordaro, who has been involved in the teddy bear world for many years. *Courtesy Gund.*

Right: Walt Disney®'s beloved bear *Winnie-the-Pooh* and Gund have a long relationship dating back to the 1960s when Disney® adapted the classic A.A. Milne stories into animated featurettes. Gund produced a plush *Winnie-the-Pooh* and a *Christopher Robin* vinyl doll in the late 1960s. From 1970 to 1993 Gund produced the Disney® *Winnie-the-Pooh* exclusively for Sears, Roebuck & Company. Commencing in 1994, Gund is the licensee for the classic *Winnie-the-Pooh* and Friends based on the Milne stories and original E. H. Shepard drawings. Pictured is Gund's magnificent 1994 rendition of this beloved bear character. *Courtesy Gund.*

Below: Artist and sculptor Gisele Nash, creator of the *Cinnabears.*

Inspired by the stories and drawings of Gisele Nash, Gund has brought to life the *Cinnabears* (1994). A wholesome family, originally sculpted by Gisele. The *Cinnabears* are fully jointed mixed-media bear sculptures. Set in bodies of soft plush, these bears have finely sculpted vinyl face masks. They have the sweet-spicy fragrance of cinnamon as their family name indicates. The family includes *Nana Nutmeg*; *Grandpa Basil*; their son *Herb*; *Herb's* wife *Clove*; their three children *Dill*, *Rosemary* and *Parsley*, and *Herb's* sea-faring brother, *Uncle Salty* with his pet seagull *Cecile*. Packaged with *Dill* and *Rosemary* are two adorable little *Cinnaberries*. *Courtesy Gund*.

Left: The attractive display box for the *Cinnabears*. (Please refer to page 80 for information regarding the *Cinnabears*). Artistically designed and illustrated by original creator of the *Cinnabears*, Gisele Nash, inside each box is the story of the *Cinnabears*, together with the family portraits. Inside display box is *Clove* holding baby *Parsley*. *Courtesy Gund.*

Right: After considerable persuasion on Auntie Linda's part, my nephew Scott Parris agreed to pose with Canterbury Bears' handsome creation *Herbert* (distributed by Gund)... a masculine looking bear even a boy could warm up to!

Knickerbocker Toy Company

The Knickerbocker Toy Company, which took its name from the traditional nickname for New York inhabitants, originated in New York as a manufacturer and seller of stuffed dolls, animals, toy puppets, marionettes and mechanical toys. In the 1960s, Smokey Bear was one of their specialties. One talks on tape and repeats eight different sentences. One notable characteristic of Knickerbocker teddy bears was the use of extremely high quality mohair. Hence the slogan attached to all their products: "Toys of Distinction." In the year 1979, the company was sold to Lionel, which underwent bankruptcy in 1984. The company was resurrected by a family with — coincidentally — the same name of Knickerbocker which began marketing a quality line of Knickerbocker products in January of 1990.

Left: Knickerbocker. Bear. Circa 1930. 20in (51cm); dark brown mohair; black button eyes; jointed arms and legs; swivel head; excelsior stuffing. Wide head and large round ears denote a Knickerbocker design. Rare to find with original box. *Courtesy of Sherryl Shirran.*

Below: Knickerbocker Toy Co., New York City pictured a wide range of stuffed animals in a *Playthings* 1927 advertisement. Featured in the ad was *Billy* the Lucky Pup. *Courtesy* Playthings *Magazine.*

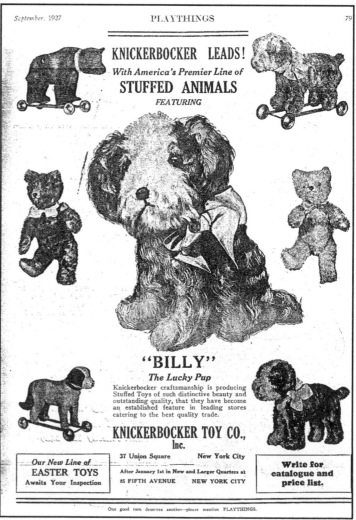

Above left: Knickerbocker. Bear. Circa 1930. 17in (43cm); bright gold silky mohair; glass eyes; realistic black metal nose; body is stuffed with Kapok; head stuffed with excelsior. Although unmarked this bear has characteristics which can be attributed to Knickerbocker's design: round head; short muzzle; large cupped round ears; small oval feet; no claws. Bright gold mohair was a prevalent color in Knickerbocker bears produced during the 1930s and 1940s. *Courtesy Susie Carlson.*

Above right: Knickerbocker Toy Co. Bear. Circa 1940; 14in (36cm); long silky gold mohair; short mohair inset snout; short mohair tops of feet; felt lined open mouth; glass eyes; jointed arms and legs; swivel head; excelsior stuffing. Note: Downturned paws gives appearance of bear cub. Cardboard lined feet enables bear to stand. Label sewn into front seam reads: "Knickerbocker Toy Co., New York." *Courtesy Wisconsin River Collection.*

Right: Knickerbocker Toy Co. Bear. Circa 1940; 13in (34cm); long white silky mohair; short, white mohair inset snout; felt paw pads; amber glass eyes; jointed arms and legs; swivel head; body stuffed with Kapok; head stuffed with excelsior. Label stitched in front seam reads: "Animals of Distinction/Made in U.S.A." reverse of label reads "Knickerbocker Toy Co., New York." Knickerbocker also sewed the labels into the side seams of their bears. Note large round head, short snout, large cupped ears; short, chubby body; fairly short chunky arms and legs; round feet and no claws. These are all distinguishing features of Knickerbocker bears produced during the 1940s compared to the earlier more slender design (page 82, top). *Courtesy Susie Carlson.*

Left: Knickerbocker Toy Co. Bear. Circa 1940; 13in (34cm); rich cinnamon-colored long silky mohair; short inset beige velveteen snout and paw pads; glass eyes; jointed arms and legs; swivel head; body stuffed with Kapok; head stuffed with excelsior. Knickerbocker produced bears with velveteen inset snouts and paw pads in bright colors of gold and brown mohair during the 1940s. This bear represents one of Knickerbocker's primary designs during the 1940s. *Courtesy Susie Carlson.*

Below: Knickerbocker Toy Co., Inc. Pouting Bears. Circa 1955. (Left to right, 15in [38cm], 6in [15cm], 10in [25cm]); vinyl faces and ears with hand-painted features; acrylic plush unjointed bodies; stationary heads. Label reads: "Pouting Animals"/Knickerbocker Toy Co., Inc." *Courtesy Pat Todd.*

Knickerbocker Bear. 1969. 8in (22cm); deep gold plush; white plush inset snout; plastic eyes; jointed arms and legs; swivel head; cotton stuffing. Made for Long Island Doll, Hobby and Craft Club, Inc. Indian Summer Party 10-26-69. Tag in back seam reads: "Joy of a Toy Company, Inc./ Middlesex, N.J. U.S.A." Rare to find with original box. *Courtesy Sue and Randal Foskey. Photograph by Randal Foskey.*

Knickerbocker Bear Company. *Mrs. Knickerbocker's Workshop.* 1993. Designed for the 1993 Disneyland® Teddy Bear and Doll Classic One-of-a-Kind Teddy Bear Auction. *Courtesy Knickerbocker Bear Company.*

Character

Character Novelty Co. thrived for more than thirty years under the leadership of two New Yorkers, Caesar Mangiapani and Jack Levy, who established the stuffed-toy company in 1932. The business really took off after the Second World War, when it began producing a wide range of animals, including teddy bears. The toys were designed by Mangiapani and Levy managed all the sales. Major department stores were its major clients. Jack Levy retired in 1960, but Novelty continued successfully until 1983 when Caesar Mangiapani died.

Above:. Character Novelty Co. Musical Bear. Circa 1930. 15in (38cm); rich cinnamon-colored mohair; glass eyes; jointed arms and legs; swivel head; kapok stuffing. Label attached to left ear reads "Character Novelty Co." Music box encased in tummy plays "Toy Maker's Dream." High forehead; shaved muzzle; fairly large ears (inner edge of ear stitched into facial seam); no stitched claws (occasionally claws were airbrushed onto paw and foot pads); manufacturers label stitched into ear seam, all are typical of Character bears from this era. *Courtesy Susie Carlson.*

Right: Character Novelty Co. Bear. Circa 1960; 12in (31cm); white mohair; glass eyes; jointed arms and legs; swivel head; kapok stuffing. Label sewn in left ear reads: "Character Novelty Co., Inc., S. Norwalk, Conn." The oversized head gives the appearance of a baby bear. Note painted claws on paw pads. The majority of Character bears have their identification tag sewn into left ear. *Courtesy Susie Carlson.*

Above: Commonwealth Toy and Novelty Co., Inc. *Bialosky Treasury of Teddy Bears*. 1995. The Treasury is a collection of nostalgic bears designed by Alan, Peggy and Jeffrey Bialosky. Ranging in sizes from 6in (17cm) to 21in (53cm) the bears are acrylic plush, fully jointed with plastic eyes, and come in limited editions of up to 2,500. *Courtesy Commonwealth Toy and Novelty Co., Inc.*

Above: Sue Coe has been collecting bears made by the Character Novelty Company for 10 years (1984). Her bears range in size from 12in (31cm) to 16in (41cm). Earlier Character bears have the manufacturer's label sewn into the left ear. Identifiable marks of the cute baby-faced bears are a red felt tongue; white felt circles behind eyes and unjointed bodies (earlier versions were fully jointed). *Courtesy Sue Coe.*

Right: (Left and Right) Commonwealth Toy and Novelty Co. *Feed Me Bears*. Circa 1937. ([Left] 16in [41cm]; cinnamon-colored mohair; [right] 13in [33cm] gold mohair); glass eyes; unjointed arms and legs; stationary head; when ring located on top of head is pulled the mouth opens and dry foods and candy are swallowed. The food can be removed by opening a zipper at the back of the bear, disclosing a metal compartment where the food is stored, without harming the bear. Originally came with a bib and a lunch box. The National Biscuit Co., used the bears to advertise their animal crackers. (Center) Commonwealth Toy Co. Musical Bear. Circa 1960. 15in (38cm); brown synthetic plush; white synthetic plush inset snout; unjointed body; stationary head. Music is produced by key located at back of torso.

Commonwealth Toy & Novelty Co., Inc.

Commonwealth Toy & Novelty Co., Inc. is one of the oldest and largest stuffed toy companies in the world today. Founded in 1934, the New York City-based company consistently markets a product of high quality and unique design.

Their plush toys are well-known through major U.S. promotions with companies such as Burger King, Nikon, Nabisco and Proctor & Gamble, to name a few.

Some of Commonwealth's better known retailer promotions include Velveteen Rabbit with Toys "R" Us, Earth Angel Bear, with Venture Stores and Christmas Bearable Bear with Gottchalks Department Stores.

The company employs 85 people and serves not only this country, but international markets worldwide. Its expertise is in manufacturing and design. Commonwealth employs a network of 30 factories in six countries to produce its wares.

Mary Meyer Stuffed Toys

The Mary Meyer story is another family business success story. At 89, this company's founder still loves to sew! Mary and her husband Hans started their company in 1933. He sold and she sewed. In 1947, along with their two children, the Meyers moved to Townshend, Vermont and have never moved.

During those years, following in the footsteps of Marguerite Steiff, Mary Meyer built an entire menagerie of stuffed animal designs, including dogs and cats, monkeys, and elephants. The teddy bear is still the number one stuffed toy and there are thousands of variations in the teddy bear's design.

Today Mary Meyer, her son Walter and grandsons operate and manage the business. Grandson Kevin is the President. Grandson Steven manages the design department and Grandson Michael is responsible for the warehousing and distributing of hundreds of thousands of stuffed toys.

Right: Mary Meyer, founder of Mary Meyer Stuffed Toys sits at the fireside of her Vermont home with a 1994 *Green Mountain Bear*. On November 15, 1993 Mary Meyer, also affectionately known as "Gram" celebrated her 90th birthday and 61 years of contribution to the teddy bear world. *Courtesy Mary Meyer Stuffed Toys.*

Left: Mary Meyer Stuffed Toys celebrates its milestone anniversary with the limited edition *60th Anniversary Bear*. (1993). The beautiful 18in (46cm) bear is fully jointed and wears an exquisite cut velvet dress. Each of the 2,000 pieces has its number in the series embroidered on a footpad. The other footpad features a Mary Meyer commemorative ribbon. The *60th Anniversary Bear* is packaged in an attractive collectible box. *Courtesy Mary Meyer Stuffed Toys.*

Early stuffed toys made by Mary Meyer were covered in gingham and stuffed with cotton. They appear in antique shops, collections and also in the homes of some employees who saved sample products over the years. Modern Mary Meyer toys have changed considerably.

The coverings used today are predominantly plush or imitation fur fabrics. During World War II, the company even used remnants of Army Camouflage materials. Today the family searches for the best, most beautiful fabrics made and incorporates them into the fine stuffed toys that sell in retail stores in all 50 states and foreign countries.

Mary Meyer Stuffed Toys. *The Green Mountain Bears.* 1994. (Top) White plush 15in (38cm) fully jointed bear with green and white knitted stocking cap. (Bottom row left and right) *Mansfield*; dark brown plush. *Bolton*; beige plush. All three bears (bottom of picture) are 9in (23cm); fully jointed; have black plastic eyes and wear green and white knitted sweaters. Each of the *Green Mountain Bears* are named after well-known Vermont mountains, and are designed by Vermont bear artist, Carol Carini. *Courtesy Mary Meyer Stuffed Toys.*

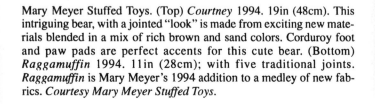

Mary Meyer Stuffed Toys. (Top) *Courtney* 1994. 19in (48cm). This intriguing bear, with a jointed "look" is made from exciting new materials blended in a mix of rich brown and sand colors. Corduroy foot and paw pads are perfect accents for this cute bear. (Bottom) *Raggamuffin* 1994. 11in (28cm); with five traditional joints. *Raggamuffin* is Mary Meyer's 1994 addition to a medley of new fabrics. *Courtesy Mary Meyer Stuffed Toys.*

Applause, Inc.

Applause Inc., a world leader in the gift industry, is home to some of the best known merchandising licenses in the country. The Woodland Hills, California-based company holds the rights to popular characters from Disney®, Sesame Street®, Looney Tunes, Tiny Toons, Raggedy Ann and Andy, and many more. More than 55,000 retailers nationwide purchase some of the most recognizable gift merchandise in the country from this thriving, privately-held company.

In 1982, Wallace Berrie and Co., Inc. acquired the Applause division from Knickerbocker Toys. In 1987, the company changed its name to Applause Inc., and acquired several classic licenses such as Disney® and Sesame Street®.

An extremely popular Applause line is the Raikes Bears. When bear artist Robert Raikes first approached Applause,

the company was hesitant. After looking through some photographs, interest was peaked and it was acknowledged that the Raikes bears were the most exciting and fresh product to come around for quite awhile. The unique partnership between Raikes and Applause became official in 1984.

Today, Applause Inc. has expanded into many divisions. Applause gift dominates the plush, figurine, and infant/toddler categories of the gift industry. It is also a formidable presence in the ceramic home decor and collectible areas. These divisions are marketed by one of the largest direct sales forces in the U.S. gift industry. Applause's International division markets the Applause product line through distributors in more than 45 countries.

Applause Inc. *Teddy Tum Tum* Bears 1993 (Left to right) Safari, Sailor and Aviator. 13in (33cm); beige acrylic plush; plastic eyes; unjointed. *Courtesy Bears in the Attic, Reisterstown, Maryland.*

The Raikes *Circus Collection* by Applause. 1993-1994. (Left to right.) *The Ringmaster*, *Maurice the Monkey*, *Addison* and *Emma* the Circus Attend- ees; *Violet the Pig* and *Bailey the Clown*. Limited edition of 5,000 each. *Courtesy Applause Inc.*

Robert Raikes, 1994 Christmas Editions by Applause. (Right to left.) *Kringle Bear*. 15in (38cm); white plush; carved wooden face; foot and paw pads; plastic eyes; fully jointed body; red burgundy velvet costume. Limited edition of 5,000 pieces. *Snowflake Reindeer with Sleigh. Snowflake*. 13in (33cm) tall; white plush; carved wooden face, antlers and feet; plastic eyes; unjointed body. Limited edition of 5,000 pieces. *The Christmas Crafts- men*. Three craftsmen (bears) are *Rembrandt* with his paintbrush, *Sawyer* with his saw and *Tinker* with his hammer. Each measures approximately 8in (20cm) tall. These three bears are boxed as a single set. Limited edition of 5,000 each set. *Courtesy Applause Inc.*

Dakin, Inc.

Founded in 1955 by Richard Y. Dakin, Dakin, Inc. is now a leading manufacturer and distributor of classic, branded plush (stuffed animals) and licensed characters to gift and toy stores world wide. Headquartered in the San Francisco Bay Area, the company's product development and marketing offices are located in Woodland Hills. Dakin stuffed animals are manufactured in the Far East and sold in over 50 countries.

The company employs more than 100 people in the United States and an independent sales force which totals more than 100 representatives. With facilities in Belgium, England, Canada, Australia and Mexico, Dakin markets its products around the world.

Dakin provides more than 1,000 quality, branded plush products at popular prices to more than 50,000 retailers including gift and specialty shops, department stores and toy stores.

Left: Robert (Bob) G. Solomon, chairman and chief executive officer of Dakin, Inc. since January 1992, is credited with reorganizing Dakin's management team and is responsible for revitalizing the company. *Courtesy Dakin.*

Below: A representation of Dakin's most popular products featured at the 1993 Toy Fair in New York. *Courtesy Dakin.*

Left: Dakin *Pierre* Carnival Bear 1991. 16in (41cm); pale cream acrylic plush head and paws; clown outfit an integral part of body; plastic eyes; jointed arms and legs; swivel head. *Courtesy Bears in the Attic, Reisterstown, Maryland.*

Below: Dakin *Patches* teddy bear. 1994. Dakin manufacturers more than 900 classic branded plush (stuffed animals). *Courtesy Dakin.*

Some of its products include seasonal merchandise designed for primary holidays and licensed characters such as Garfield and Clifford the Big Red Dog. In addition to its best-selling toy line, Dakin markets the successful Ginny Doll.

Dakin's most recent coup is its role as the sole licensed plush source for Barney merchandise. This beloved prehistoric reptile has hit the children's market by storm. In 1992, Dakin introduced a variety of assorted plush styles and puppets for both Barney and his side-kick, Baby Bop. According to Sheryl Leach, President of The Lyon's Group, the Dallas based company is excited to be working with Dakin. "In our minds, Dakin is the premier plush company in the industry. We've been aware of the wonderful product they've developed for other licensed properties over the years. We're thrilled to have them on board."

Dakin's management team is led by Bob Solomon (Chairman, CEO and President) and Jack Morrow (Executive Vice President).

Charleen Kinser Designs

Charleen Kinser was born, grew up and attended school in Long Beach, California. After studying for two years at Chouinard Art Institute in Los Angeles, she went to work in the field of movie animation with U.P.A. She designed backgrounds and characters, eventually becoming a director. Her career took her to London where she directed TV commercials and eventually she claimed three Cannes Festival Awards while at Les Cineastes in Paris. As she accompanied her husband, Bill, around the United States, she continued working as a free lance designer. Eventually Bill accepted a position at Penn State University and the Kinsers and their two children settled in Pennsylvania.

The entire family got involved in the toy business. Bill is the graphic designer. Daughter Maggie develops many of the characters through her whimsical writing and son Tom has designed and made wooden toys. The business is centered in a 100-year-old Pennsylvania bank barn. A small group does all of the cutting, stuffing and finishing. Everything is hand done. Old treadle sewing machines are used. Most of the handsewing is done by people with little shops or studios.

Extensive research goes into all the characters produced by Charleen Kinser Designs. The company's objective is to make the best designed and produced toys available. The success of their goal is manifested in simple, timeless toys, designed to "intrigue children, to withstand their play and to provide beautiful handmade toys that are theirs alone." Every gesture and detail are the stuff on which imaginations can soar.

Charleen Kinser works with a small group of artisans in an old bank barn in central Pennsylvania. Charleen says they have a good time together, however their main objective is to make the best designed and produced toys as possible; toys with personalities, an extension of the characters already in a persons mind to ensure a part in dreams and melodramas.

Charleen Kinser Designs. *Roving Bear.* 1987. 18in (46cm); brown Belgian sheepskin (natural color); glass eyes; polyester stuffing covers pine wooden body; hand-sewn leather nose; plastic claws; painted cherry wood rockers. Riding the bear is Charleen Kinser's popular Gnome *Tom Griswold II.* Deerskin head, hands and feet; acrylic hair; glass eyes; polyester and cotton body; jointed head and legs; dangling arms. *Courtesy Charleen Kinser Designs. Photograph by George Hornbein.*

Charleen Kinser Designs. *The Storybook Bear.* 1989. 18in (46cm); tan imported acrylic plush; glass eyes; nose and paw pads hand-stitched pigskin; jointed arms and legs; swivel head. *Courtesy Charleen Kinser Designs. Photograph by Bruce Cramer.*

Above: Charleen Kinser Designs. (Left to right) *T.R.'s Bear's Cub.* 1978. 24in (61cm); variegated brown acrylic plush; glass eyes; unjointed; hand-stitched cowhide nose. (Center) *Baby Bear.* 1979. 18in (46cm); variegated brown acrylic plush; glass eyes; loose plush skin over jointed body; hand-stitched cowhide nose and leather foot pads. (Right) *T.R.'s Bear.* 1977. 60in (152cm); variegated brown acrylic plush; glass eyes; cowhide nose. The adorable little girl feeding the baby bear signifies *Goldilocks and the Three Bears. Courtesy Charleen Kinser Designs. Photograph by Jacqueline Baer.*

Right: Charleen Kinser Designs. The very first *T.R.'s Bear* (1977) with neighborhood friend. *Courtesy Charleen Kinser Designs.*

North American Bear Co., Inc.

In the mid 1970s, while raising a small child and studying ceramic and toy design, Barbara Isenberg started a toy company to produce uniquely designed, high quality teddy bears. The bears had the nostalgic charm of antique toys, with an appeal for both children and adults. Barbara asked her friend, Odl Bauer, a fashion designer, to make a bear out of an old sweatshirt that would be soft, cuddly and different from anything else on the market. That bear evolved into Albert the Running Bear, now a classic bear in a colorful running suit. In 1978 she teamed up with her brother Paul Levy to form the North American Bear Company. Today Paul heads up finance, sales and the warehouses located in Chicago. Barbara Isenberg heads up the New York Studio where all the products are created by an in-house team of designers and artists. The most well-known North American Bear Co. lines are the VIB line, the VanderBear Family and Muffy VanderBear.

It was in 1983 that the company decided to do an entire family of bears, and thus the VanderBears came about. The next year, little Muffy was born, wearing a christening gown. By 1988 she had practically become the *Barbie®* or *Madame Alexander* of the teddy bear world. She has her own fan club

Left: The success of Barbara Isenberg, founder of the world renown North American Bear Company is overwhelming. It truly shows how a small creative endeavor can grow into a full-scale business. Barbara (center of front row) is pictured in her New York design studio surrounded by her creative staff who Barbara says contribute so much to the success of her company. *Courtesy North American Bear Co., Inc.*

Right: North American Bear Company. *V.I.P.s* ("Very Important Bears"). This line of celebrity bears was one of the company's first success stories. Introduced in 1979 by Barbara Isenberg (the first was *Amelia Bearhart* and *Douglas Bearbanks*), these bears with unusual faces, vivid skin colors, lavish costumes and punning names quickly found a following that has remained loyal to this day. There are now approximately 20 *V.I.B.s* available and 51 retired bears that enjoy a successful collectible status. *Courtesy North American Bear Co., Inc.*

Above left: North American Bear Company., Inc. *Muffy VanderBear* and *Hoppy VanderHare*: "Yankee Doodle." Introduced Spring 1992. *Muffy* and *Hoppy* look fine and dandy in their red, white and blue 4th of July finery. *Muffy Yankee Doodle* wears a colonial frock with feathered hat and *Hoppy Uncle Sam* steps lively in her top hat, rompers and tails. Both wear lace-up shoes. *Courtesy North American Bear Co., Inc.*

Above right: North American Bear Co., Inc. *V.I.B.s* ("Very Important Bears"). "The Wizard of Paws." *Judy Bearland.* 1993. 20in (51cm); in her classic role as Dorothy from "The Wizard of Paws", Judy follows the yellow brick road in her trademark ruby slippers. With Toto cradled in her arms she wears her blue-and-white gingham dress with puffed sleeves and matching head bows. *Courtesy North American Bear Co., Inc.*

Right: North American Bear Company., Inc. *Muffy VanderBear* and *Hoppy VanderHare*: "Rainy Day." Introduced Fall 1992. *Courtesy North American Bear Co., Inc.*

with thousands of members and even appears in the annual Macy's Thanksgiving Day Parade in New York City.

North American Bear also provides a complete array of accessories and collateral material accompanying little Muffy, including a tea set, table and chair, sofa, cupboard, steamer trunk and even stationery.

Barbara Isenberg prides herself, and her company on team work. As she said in *Teddy Bear Review®* (May/June 1992), "you don't hear the word 'I' tossed around much here; 'we' is the key, and for good reason."

Illustration 215. North American Bear Co., Inc. *Cornelius* and *Muffy VanderBear.* "Cherry Pie: The Baking Collection—Daddy and Me at the Patisserie VdeB." Introduced Spring 1992. *Courtesy North American Bear Co., Inc.*

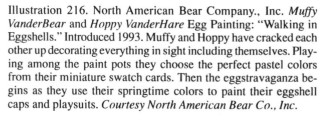

Illustration 216. North American Bear Company., Inc. *Muffy VanderBear* and *Hoppy VanderHare* Egg Painting: "Walking in Eggshells." Introduced 1993. Muffy and Hoppy have cracked each other up decorating everything in sight including themselves. Playing among the paint pots they choose the perfect pastel colors from their miniature swatch cards. Then the eggstravaganza begins as they use their springtime colors to paint their eggshell caps and playsuits. *Courtesy North American Bear Co., Inc.*

North American Bear Company., Inc. The Vander-Bear Family. "A Taste O' Honey: The VdBee Keeping Collection." Introduced Spring 1993. Sporting traditional black stripes on sturdy cotton mattress ticking, *Cornelius, Alice, Fuzzy and Fluffy* are adorned with custom bee-themed woven labels and "VdeB" - monogrammed provincial neckerchiefs. *Muffy* and *Hoppy* are adorably costumed as honeybee and ladybug. *Courtesy North American Bear Co., Inc.*

North American Bear Company., Inc. "Bear Market." A wonderful array of the appealing cuddly plush bears and rabbits produced by this world-renowned company. *Courtesy North American Bear Co., Inc.*

Above: (Right) R. John Wright. *Pocket Pooh.* 1993. 5in (13cm); gold mohair; black button-type eyes; jointed arms and legs; swivel head; short deep red waistcoat. Limited edition 3,500. (Left) R. John Wright. *Pocket Piglet.* 1994. 2in (6cm); pink felt; black button-type eyes; jointed arms and legs; swivel head; green felt body suit an integral part of body. Limited edition of 3,500. *Courtesy R. John Wright.*

Left: American doll and teddy bear artist R. John Wright's highly collectible creation of *Christopher Robin* and *Winnie-the-Pooh* have won the hearts of numerous collectors throughout America. (Left) *Christopher Robin.* 1985. 18in (46cm); 100% wool felt; painted facial features; fully jointed; blue cotton jacket; brown cotton shorts; white cotton hat; brown leather shoes. (Right) *Winnie-the-Pooh.* 1985. 8in (20cm); caramel-colored custom-made 100% wool; "coating" black glass eyes; jointed arms and legs; swivel heads; knit jacket. Sold originally as a set. Limited edition 1,000 each. *Photograph by Larry McDaniel.*

R. John Wright Dolls, Inc.

Ten years ago, John Wright's Christopher Robin and Winnie-the-Pooh were named as Doll of the Year by the readers of *Doll Reader® Magazine* and the United Federation of Doll Clubs.

Now R. John Wright Dolls, based in upstate Cambridge, New York is making headlines with its tiny "Pocket Pooh" and other characters from the beloved Winnie-the-Pooh stories. (Top right of this page.) The diminutive 5in (13cm) Pooh was the hottest selling bear of 1993, selling out 3,500 pieces in only six weeks.

The Pocket Collection is faithfully based on the original classic illustrations by E.H. Shepard capturing their nostalgia and style. They are numbered for authenticity and beautifully boxed in the R. John Wright traditions.

Since the Christopher Robin and Winnie-the-Pooh series is licensed by Disney®, these items are also available through the Disney® stores and theme parks.

Most of the creations produced by this small company are of molded felt with just a few workers at their home/factory. Some clothing and accessories are "farmed out" to people who work in their homes. John and his wife, Susan, still paint most of the facial features, style the hair, and mold the faces.

Bearly People

Cheryle de Rose started dressing teddy bears as a hobby. After a year of successful teddy bear shows, she incorporated Bearly People in 1983. The Bearly People Bears have adorable faces and are jointed so they can be posed. Cheryle says she prefers the old-fashioned way of dressing bears. Every dress is completely sewn by one person, not passed around an assembly line. According to Cheryle de Rose "you cannot rush the process when you are making a truly collectible teddy bear."

Cheryl DeRose, Bearly People. *Bunny's Pansy Patch*. Bear. 1992. 18in (46cm); beige synthetic plush; plastic eyes; jointed arms and legs; swivel head. Dressed in a pansy print dress with straw hat trimmed with pansies. A little white rabbit peeks out of a pansy-filled basket. *Courtesy Bearly People. Photograph by Wes Isbutt.*

Cheryl DeRose, Bearly People. (Left) *Lazy "J" Wrangler,* (right) *Sweet Virginia*. Bears. 1992. 16in (41cm); beige synthetic plush; plastic eyes; jointed arms and legs; swivel head. Their brightly colored outfits represent the popular theme of the "Southwest Bears" collection. *Courtesy Bearly People. Photograph by Wes Isbutt.*

Hotchkin Bear Company

Bonnie Hotchkin began as most bear artists do, by making gifts for others. The Kin Bears were born when she made each of her granddaughter's their own teddy bear. Aware that the last three letters of her last name, "Kin", meant family, Bonnie used this to name her bear line. In fact, Bonnie named eight of the ten original Kin Bears in the "Heart of Gold" booklet after her two sons, granddaughters and sisters. The one named after her only grandson, Christopher was introduced at Toy Fair 1992.

Bonnie Hotchkin officially entered the commercial teddy bear world with a "Meet the Artist" in 1987. And, as she says "life was never the same after that."

The company's 1990 Golden Teddy Award winner "Alas'kin" was retired in 1992 due to the death of a gentleman who hand-caned the snow shoes for just $6 pair. He told Bonnie that the shoes were great therapy for him in his fight against cancer. Since then, the lowest price quoted to the company has been $30. These shoes are just a representation of the intricate works of art that go into a Hotchkin bear.

Bonnie J. Hotchkin and the two *Golden Teddy* winners along with her bear *Christopher* introduced at the 1992 New York Toy Fair. *Alas' kin.* 19" (48cm) (wearing snow shoes). *Patch' kin.* 19" (48cm) pink, blue, cream bear. *Christopher* in sunglasses 15in (38cm). *Courtesy Bonnie J. Hotchkin. Photograph by "Studio Boris."*

"Kin" Bears designed by Bonnie J. Hotchkin have a gold heart on their chest, warm realistic eyes, and are made with exquisite domestic plush. A beautifully illustrated heart-shaped booklet describing the "Kin" Bears' unique personalities accompanies each bear. Pictured are three of Bonnie's most popular 1990 bears (left to right) *Belissa* 16in (41cm), *Bo* 19in (48cm); and *Granny* 21in (53cm). *Courtesy Bonnie J. Hotchkin. Photograph by Gary Newyear.*

Oz International

Remi Kramer wrote and illustrated his first children's book, *The Legend of LoneStar Bear*, after 20 years of directing and writing films in Hollywood. After the successful publication of the book, Oz Enterprises was born to produce the new bear designs which evolved from the characters of these delightful children's books. After the LoneStar Bear, came Little Moon, Teddy Rufff Rider, Bugle Boy Bear, Klondike Ike, The Cactus Kid, Buffalo Boy and a host of other unique creations. The LoneStar Bear books have been cited for The Top 100 Products of the Year Award and were honored by *Creativity* '90 for "Best Illustration." Twice a winner of the Golden Teddy Award, Kramer's bears were nominated for both the Golden Teddy Award and The TOBY® Award in 1992.

Right: Remi Kramer proudly holds his 1990 Golden Teddy Award-winning bear *Little Moon* (right) and his popular *Lonestar Bear. Courtesy Remi Kramer.*

Below left: Remi Kramer, Oz International. *Lonestar Bear.* 1989. (Foreground 16in [41cm]) background 10in (25cm); honey-colored plush; plastic eyes; jointed arms and legs; swivel head. Dressed in brown hat, boots, fringed vest and red bandanna. *Courtesy Remi Kramer.*

Below right: Remi Kramer, Oz International. *Good Ol' Tom.* 1991. 18in (46cm); honey-colored mohair; glass eyes; jointed arms and legs; swivel head. Wearing white ultrasuede hat with hand-loomed beaded hat band, fringed buckskin gloves, Mongolian sheepskin chaps with sterling silver buckle, custom made bandanna. *Courtesy Remi Kramer.*

Cooperstown Bears. *1869 Cincinnati Red Stockings* 125th Anniversary Bear. On May 4, 1869 the Cincinnati Red Sockings, America's first professional baseball team took the field. That day the Cincinnati club won and continued its streak for 84 consecutive games. In the 125 years that have followed, baseball has brought joy to generations of fans. Cooperstown Bears celebrated this historical event by producing the *1869 Cincinnati Red Stockings* bear in a 1994 limited edition of 1,000. *Courtesy Cooperstown Bears.*

Cooperstown Bears, Ltd.

Cooperstown Bears, Ltd. was founded because Robert Kronenberger couldn't find a high quality souvenir for his children while attending a baseball game. Kronenberger, President of Cooperstown Bears and American Needle, Inc., is the third generation of Kronenbergers to head this family business which was started in 1918 by his grandfather Ike as a baseball cap company.

The marriage of two great American favorites — baseball and teddy bears — has produced a wonderful line of specialty collectibles. Beginning with the company's first edition of a set of 12 uniformed 21in (54cm) Cooperstown Bears, the company has since added 16in (41cm) bears in brown or ivory plush with 16 teams from which to choose. The first edition, which is nearly sold out, was limited to only 2,500 pieces world wide. That original run offers a nostalgic view of the changes in styles over the years for each team.

The company also offers customers the opportunity to collect bears in the recognizable uniforms of today (or "diamond" uniforms as the official Major League nomenclature calls them).

Cooperstown also has produced a distinctive line of 100% mohair, limited edition bears such as the Babe Ruth Teddy, whose chubby body, wide set eyes and broad snout resemble the great home run hitter himself. He comes complete with an authentic Yankees uniform of his era and a "bear-sized" Louisville Slugger bat. This bear was nominated for the Golden Teddy Award. Only 1,000 were produced.

Another historic piece is the tall, thin, "Shoeless" Joe Jackson, who wears the 1917 Chicago White Sox uniform and comes with his own "Black Betsy," his favorite bat.

Cooperstown Bears honored the 125th Anniversary of America's Favorite Pastime with a special mohair teddy, wearing the same ivory, long sleeved uniform with bib front that the Cincinnati Red Stockings first wore in 1869.

The Cooperstown Teddy Collection is a nostalgic look back at two of America's most endearing favorites - teddy bears and baseball. Each bear in the Cooperstown Collection is 21in (55cm) tall and is created in the style of an original turn-of-the-century teddy, exquisitely reproduced by hand. The authentic uniform quality of the Cooperstown Teddy honors the past in all of its glory. The makers of this quality collection were chosen for their extreme attention to detail. They are the only company in America commissioned to create this valuable series. Each authentically reproduced team uniform is designed from original sources, historical documents, photographs and detailed information from famed baseball historians. *Courtesy Cooperstown Bears.*

The Boyds Collection Ltd.

Gary and Tina Lowenthal's entree into the world of teddy bears came through an antique shop in the rural town of Boyds, Maryland. It was in this small shop that they began to wholesale some of the antique reproductions they sold. In 1982, duck decoys were the mainstay of the Boyds Collection. Gary painted, antiqued, packaged, sold and shipped the creations, while Tina took care of customer service, billing and accounting. Soon, as more staff were added, wool teddy bears and miniature resin houses were part of the mix. Five years later, the company moved to Littlestown, Pennsylvania. That same year, 1987, Gae Sharp, designer of Hudson, the original beanbag bear, signed a licensing agreement with Gary Lowenthal

and Boyds began producing this talented artist's beanbag bears, rabbits, cats and dogs. When Gae Sharp fell ill the next year, Gary was forced to take over the design of the plush line which is now a conglomeration of a number of themes and ideas. Gae Sharp's line of jointed, bean-bag style animals is called "J.B. Bean and Associates." Other lines are entitled "The Archive Collection," "T.J.'s Best Dressed," "Bears in the Attic," and "The Artist Bear." The Boyds Collection also offers peripheral items such as furniture, clothing and accessories called "Bear Necessities." The Boyds Collection is particularly noted for providing affordable, yet highly collectible works.

Right: Peeking over Gary Lowenthals' (founder of The Boyds Collection Ltd.) shoulder is one of the numerous appealing bears produced by this rapidly growing company. *Courtesy The Boyds Collection Ltd.*

Below: The appealing bears and animals in The Boyds Collection are developed around different themes and ideas. The jointed and pellet-filled bodies can be posed in a wide variety of positions. *Courtesy The Boyds Collection Ltd.*

The Vermont Teddy Bear Co.

John Sortino founded The Vermont Teddy Bear Company when he noticed all the teddy bears his son received were made overseas. John felt that the teddy bear was an American invention, so he decided to create, sew and sell teddy bears. He began by selling his bears from a cart and listened carefully to his customers. This kept him developing new designs. In 1983 he started a production company. As the company kept expanding, he hired a designer who could take his designs even further. In 1990 Kathleen Straube joined The Vermont Teddy Bear Co. and she's been designing Vermont teddy bears and their outfits ever since. Last year, the company produced 190,000 plush bears and 2000 mohair bears. The company went public in 1993.

The Vermont Teddy Bear Team. (Left to right) Kathleen Straube (bear designer), Barbara Haase (marketing director), Spence Putnam, (chief financial officer), John Sortino (founder and President), and Jane Campbell (systems manager and head of accounting). *Courtesy The Vermont Teddy Bear Company. Photograph by Rob Swanson.*

Vermont Teddy Bear Company. *Amelia.* 1992. 14in (36cm); gold mohair; plastic safety eyes; jointed arms and legs; swivel head. Designed by Kathleen Straube. *Courtesy Vermont Teddy Bear Company. Photograph by Andy Mager.*

Chapter Four

Teddy Bear Figurines

For generations, figurines have adorned fireplace mantles, ladies' vanities, pianos, hutches and table tops. Plush animal collectors are expanding their horizons to this new area as well. Well-known figurine manufacturers such as Hummel and Heubach, are being joined by modern animal figurines.

The world of teddy bear figurines is growing in popularity for two dominant reasons: space and cost. It also broadens the horizons of bear collecting. By collecting figurines, aficionados can fill shelves with darling, hand-crafted miniature versions of unique bears; and at the same time, there is the opportunity to own valuable pieces of uniquely designed sculpture, without the major expense attached to artists bears hand-produced with costly fabrics and accessories.

To the delight of collectors everywhere, bears are appearing in myriad materials. Their popularity is noticeable in the figurines made of porcelain, china, resin, wood, clay, and even crystal.

Teddy bear figurines are gaining the same kind of acceptance as the fluffy toys which inspired them. People seem to enjoy collecting teddy bears whether they can cuddle up to them, display them or benefit from their secondary market value. A few of the most popular figurine designers and manufacturers are described below.

Enesco Corporation

One of the most respected designers and producers of fine gifts and collectibles is based in Elk Grove Village, Illinois. One man, Eugene Freedman, is credited with leading Enesco to unparalleled heights in the gift industry. The Enesco Corporation is a local industrial landmark, with more than 30,000 square feet of offices; a 455,000 square foot warehouse with state-of-the-art computerized inventory and shipping systems; and a breathtaking 35,000-square-foot showroom which undergoes two annual construction changes for the company's exclusive buyer showings. Approximately 550 administrative and office personnel and 200 union warehouse employees work at Enesco headquarters with more than 700 sales representative worldwide.

Enesco has two divisions: Enesco Designed Giftware and Enesco Gift Gallery.

Enesco Designed Giftware is responsible for the Precious Moments Collection and accessories line, Enesco Treasury of Christmas Ornaments, Sisters & Best Friends, Sesame Street® giftware, Lucy and Me, Gnomes, Sports Impressions, Tomorrow-Today, and Valentine's Day, St. Patrick's Day,

Easter and Spring product lines. Some of the best known items from this division are "Have a Beary Merry Christmas," and "Have a Beary Special Birthday," a Precious Moments birthday club gift released in 1989.

The now-famous Enesco Precious Moments Collection catapulted Enesco from being a leading gift designer and marketer to an expanded role as a leading collectible producer. Adapted from the work of inspirational artist Sam Butcher, these teardrop-eyed children with soulful expressions and inspirational messages has remained this country's number one collectible for more than a decade.

The Enesco Gift Gallery includes general giftware and other collectibles and lines such as Cherished Teddies Collection, Enesco Small World of Music Collection, Memories of Yesterday, Laura's Attic, From Barbie® with Love, Mickey & Co.,/Disney® giftware, Calico Kittens, Mary's Moo-Moos, PRO-Profitable Promotions, Star Trek, Elvis Presley, The Beatles, Saturday Night Live and Maud Humphrey Bogart Collection.

In addition to a talented staff of nearly 60 artists and designers, Enesco also markets licensed gifts and collectibles from such well-known artists as Jim Davis (Garfield), Priscilla Hillman (see page 109), Ellen Williams (Sister's and Best Friends), Lucy Rigg (see page 108), Walt Disney®, Lesley Anne Ivory (Ivory Cats), Kathy Wise and Ruth Morehead, to name a few.

Precious Moments Figurine by Enesco. "Now I lay me down to sleep and pray the Lord . . . ." 1994. 5in (14cm) high. There is nothing more precious than reading a bedtime story to a loved one. In honor of that moment, the Enesco Precious Moments Collection introduces this touching figurine. Magnificently crafted from porcelain bisque, this figurine captures a tender moment of a little boy who just finished reading a bedtime story to his trusted friend - teddy bear. *Courtesy Enesco.*

Lucy Rigg (left) has been creating her unique little bear figurines for over twenty years. Known to collectors as the Lucy and Me Company, this talented artist's first involvement with bears was while awaiting the birth of her daughter Noelle (right), Lucy chose teddy bears as the theme for Noelle's nursery. *Courtesy Lucy Rigg.*

Lucy Rigg, Enesco Lucy & Me Collection. *Chapeau Noelle.* 1994. *Joan, Linda* and *Diane* debut in the Chapeau Noelle limited edition series. All decked out in lavish hats, Chapeau Noelle (Chapeau meaning hat in French) was created by Lucy Rigg in honor of her daughter, Noelle, and reflects Lucy's love for hats. Each figurine is exquisitely sculpted out of porcelain bisque and hand-painted in soft pastel colors. Each Chapeau Noelle figurine is accompanied by a certificate of authenticity and hand signed by both Lucy and Noelle. This 1994 edition is limited to 2,000 pieces. *Courtesy Enesco.*

Lucy Rigg - Lucy and Me

While awaiting the birth of her daughter in 1969, Lucy Rigg was inspired to decorate the nursery with a theme everybody loves...teddy bears. She sculpted bears out of bakers clay and then hand painted each one. Her friends and family adored her creations and soon, she began making them for others. The next year she was selling these hand crafted bears, *Rigglets*, at street fairs...and sculpting more than 100 a day.

As Lucy told *Teddy Bear and friends*® in its May/June 1994 issue: "A lot of people ask me how I got started making bears and its not really easy to answer because it was so gradual. I first made decorations for my daughter's nursery which were bears, but the little baker's clay figures I made were really little people. I didn't start making the bears until about three or four years later."

In the late 1970s, Enesco Corporation approached Lucy at a Seattle street fair and proposed turning her bears into a line of porcelain bisque figurines and accessories. The first porcelain Rigglets were a combination of undressed bears with Lucy's identifiable red-and-white bows as well as costumed bears with themes. In 1980, Enesco formally introduced the Lucy & Me collection; since then, it has enjoyed steady support from collectors and teddy bear lovers the world over.

Lucy Rigg also owns Lucy & Me. The name evolved from the greeting card company that Lucy and Judi Jacobsen began in 1977. Judi came up with the name saying "someday Lucy and me are going to do something!" Before long, Lucy says, the teddy bear theme took over and in 1984, Lucy and Judi formed separate companies, with Lucy retaining the Lucy & Me name. Today her company produces calendars, stationary and greeting cards designed by her.

As a bear enthusiast herself, she has built a special room in her Seattle home to showcase the hundreds of Enesco Lucy & Me porcelain figurines introduced over the years. The figurines are sculpted and hand-painted overseas. But Lucy draws up most of the designs with some help from Enesco's Jeff Hutsell, Diane Stillfox, and her daughter Noelle, who is also her assistant.

The latest in the Lucy & Me collection is named after Noelle. Called "Chapeau Noelle," each of the porcelain bisque figurines are wearing large hats (which Lucy herself is also noted for wearing). These figurines are in limited editions of 2000 numbered pieces. Named after Lucy's friends, the seated bears are 5in (13cm) tall.

There seems to be endless expansion of Lucy's vision. "Lucy's Family," is a limited edition of costumed plush teddy bears produced by Jona Originals. Each bear includes a wooden stand with a brass plaque listing the collector series' name, the name of the limited edition, the date of release and the edition number.

Lucy Rigg's imagination is still hard at work producing the drawings which got her going in the beginning. Today the "Lucy Bear" concept adorns over 10,000 gift items including balloons, cards, baby books, notebooks and many more items.

There is a Lucy & Me Collecting Network which was formed to bring Lucy's collectors together. Members receive a newsletter and have the opportunity to win prizes donated by various manufacturers. They also have the opportunity to purchase exclusive merchandise.

Lucy Rigg, Enesco Lucy & Me Collection. Figurines. 1994. Lucy Rigg created something special in the Professionals Series! Each porcelain bisque figurine portrays a different profession, with each teddy bear dressing up as its respective occupation - the local fireman, nurse, teacher, dentist and many others who help make the community a neighborhood. Sizes range from 2in-3in (6cm-8cm). *Courtesy Enesco.*

Priscilla Hillman
Cherished Teddies

It was during the late 1980s that Priscilla Hillman found herself laid up for several months due to a serious back injury. These seemingly endless days of inactivity were filled with imaginary sketching and when she could finally move, Priscilla headed to the drawing board to put her dreams on paper. The Cherished Teddies were born.

Priscilla had previously illustrated and written children's books, most notably nine "Merry Mouse" books for Doubleday.

In 1990, she sent her sketches to Enesco Corporation, which introduced the giftware collection based on Priscilla's charming teddy bears in 1992.

Originally, Cherished Teddies had 16 detailed cold cast figurines. Each came with its own name and Certificate of Adoption. Today, there are more than 80 single and multiple figurines in the Collection, which is sold throughout the world. To date, more than 100,000 collectors have registered their teddy bears with the Enesco "Adoption Center." The collection now includes plush, articulated bears and gift accessories, including Post-it notes, mini plates, waterballs, ornaments and musical figurines.

Since being introduced, the collection has received worldwide recognition from collectors and the collectibles industry. The figurine "Old Friends Are the Best Friends" won a 1992 TOBY® Award from *Teddy Bear and friends*® magazine; the figurine "Friends Are Never Far Apart" won a Collec-

Priscilla Hillman, Cherished Teddies. "Friends Come In All Sizes." 1992. 2in (7cm). The adorable teddy bear trio *Theodore*, *Samantha* and *Tyler* spread their friendship to you in this resin figurine. Based on the illustrations by artist Priscilla Hillman, this figurine was one of the original sixteen pieces that was introduced in 1992. *Courtesy Enesco.*

Priscilla Hillman, award winning artist for the Enesco Cherished Teddies Collection. *Courtesy Enesco.*

tor Editions 1992 Awards of Excellence in the musicals under $100 category; "Friends Come in All Sizes" received the 1992 Giftware Association Award in the Tabletop and Collectibles category in England; the catalog group Retail Resources Inc. named the collection the 1992 Most Outstanding New Product; and Enesco's parent company, Stanhome Inc., named Cherished Teddies Product of the Year.

In 1993, the collection was named Collectible of the Year by the National Association of Limited Edition Dealers (NALED); Priscilla Hillman was also recognized as second runner up for Artist of the Year. The awards list continues to grow for these figurines which are surrounded by character and warmth.

With the success of Cherished Teddies, another collection line by Priscilla Hillman, "The Calico Kittens," was introduced in 1993.

Priscilla Hillman, Cherished Teddies. "Old Friends are the Best Friends." 1992. 5in (15cm). "Old Friends are the Best Friends" captures *Christopher* sitting by his toy chest, surrounded by some of his favorite companions. *Christopher* was one of the original 16 figurines to be introduced to the public in 1992. *Courtesy Enesco.*

Priscilla Hillman, Cherished Teddies. "Our Cherished Family." 1994. 3in (8cm) wide by 8in (20cm) tall. Dad stands up straight while Mom proudly sits on a wooden chair in these new introductions to the Cherished Teddies Collection. Little sister and brother hold on to their toys, and big sister and brother get dressed up in their Sunday best. The figurines can be posed on a house-shaped displayer that can sit or be hung for all to enjoy. Each figurine comes with a title and an official Family Member Certificate for you to name the teddy bear after someone in your own family! *Courtesy Enesco.*

Priscilla Hillman, Cherished Teddies. *Elsa*. 1994. The beautifully crafted resin Cherished Teddies Collection has won the hearts of collectors from around the world. Now, Enesco turns soft at heart by bringing collectors Cherished Teddies in plush. Soft and cuddly *Elsa* is fully jointed, has a pink bow and fabric patches. Just like the popular line of figurines, each teddy comes with its own certificate. Introduced at the same time was *Norman* (not pictured). *Norman* wears a sailor-type collar. Both bears come in three sizes: 9in (23cm), 12in (31cm) and 18in (46cm). *Courtesy Enesco.*

Sarah's Attic

While working in her husband's pharmacy, Sarah Schultz saw that the best selling products in the gift department were her own original creations of stenciled slates, boards, pictures and some dolls. As she traveled to gift shows to look for unique items for her small gift department, her tote bag brought recognition from a sales representative who suggested she start marketing her own items. After some contemplation and discussion with her husband (who is her high school sweetheart), the work of Sarah's Attic began at the dining room table.

Because Sarah is a firm believer in love, respect and dignity, a heart was painted on each piece to symbolize her trademark of quality and originality.

In 1984, the business moved from the backroom of the pharmacy to the attic directly above the drugstore. In two years, the business expanded to included resin figurines. This was the beginning of Sarah's Gang and to this day these children are an integral part of Sarah's Attic.

By Spring of 1989, the company expanded to 5000 feet of operating space and again was quickly forced to move to more space, a former grocery store with 10,000 square feet of work area. The art room, mail room, and business office still remain in the "Attic."

There are now 100 workers at the factory and more than 45 sales representatives throughout the country. Her figurines are nationally known and are available in more than 3500 stores throughout the U.S. and Canada.

Sarah Schultz began the company as a possible way of earning enough to get a new couch and now she has been able to send her four children to college and has dreams of a theme park in the Chesaning, Michigan area where she grew up and where her business flourishes.

A representation of the appealing figurines portraying teddy bears created by the renowned American company Sarah's Attic. *Courtesy Sarah's Attic.*

111

Terry & Doris Michaud - The Michaud Collection

Famous teddy bear collectors Terry and Doris Michaud are internationally recognized teddy bear experts who have produced artist bears for 15 years, authored four books and written extensively for a number of magazines. In early 1993, the two approached Sarah Schultz to propose recreating their antique bears in resin. Twelve of their favorite original bears, beginning with "The Professor," were selected to have expertly designed and sculpted resin replicas created.

Terry Michaud's concept was to take the current figurine look of "cute little bears presented in various poses and designs" to a dimension to be appreciated by collectors of greater sophistication. His idea was to bring collectors figurine replicas of their antique teddies accompanied by their stories. Sarah's Attic not only recreated the original bear, but also created a scene with the bear that relates back to the true story about the bear. The Michaud Collection from Sarah's Attic brings a sense of history and purpose to the world of contemporary collectibles.

Terry and Doris Michaud are pictured with renditions of bears from their famous antique bear collection, produced in limited editions by the Deans Co. of Great Britain. Miniature figures of bears from this wonderful collection are produced by Sarah's Attic. *Courtesy Terry and Doris Michaud.*

The Michaud Collection from Sarah's Attic. These bears are designed after the original antique teddy bears belonging to the world-famous bear collection of Terry and Doris Michaud. *Courtesy Terry and Doris Michaud.*

The Michaud Collection by Sarah's Attic. "Me and My Shadow." Figurine. 1994. Scene and single piece of "Me and My Shadow" with story card in the background. *Courtesy Terry and Doris Michaud.*

Schmid

Schmid manufactures, distributes and sells quality gifts and collectible products to retail stores. The Randolph, Massachusetts-based company began during the Depression in the basement of the family home. It was John G. Schmid's insight, and family's persistent work ethic that brought the company to its present prominent leadership position in the gift and collectible industry.

It was the discovery of Hummel figurines (from W. Goebel Porzellanfabrik Company) at a 1935 Frankfurt Fair that provided a major base for the company's sales.

As John Schmid tells it, his father predicted total disaster with the 72 Hummel figures John brought back from Germany. However, after World War II, U.S. servicemen began collecting Hummel with a vengeance and the figurines were firmly established in America.

During the 1970s, the Schmid brand came on the scene, resulting in a line of fine quality music boxes. Also, during this time frame, Schmid acquired the distribution of Border Fine Arts from Scotland which produced highly sculptured figurines.

Of course, bear collectors are drawn to Schmid's Roosevelt Bears by April Whitcomb Gustafson. This one-of-a-kind collection includes six individual sets, each featuring the fully articulated Roosevelt Bears, "Teddy B," and "Teddy G," dressed in costumes that reflect their travels around the world. Each is packaged in a miniature steamer trunk and are handcrafted of resin for fine detail and entirely hand painted.

Today, Schmid carries on its tradition of manufacturing music boxes, figurines and Christmas ornaments. Its exclusive distributorship covers the M I Hummel figurines and Walt Disney® Classics Collection (launched in 1992). Other lines include Disney® Treasures, Beatrix Potter, Thomas the Tank, Lowell Davis, Yamada, Kitty Cucumber and Gallery Two, along with Schmid's own exclusively created designs.

Schmid's Roosevelt Bears by April Whitcomb Gustafson include six individual sets, each featuring the fully articulated Roosevelt Bears, *Teddy B* and *Teddy G* dressed in costumes that reflect their travels around the world.

The bears are handcrafted of resin for fine detail and entirely hand-painted. Each Roosevelt Bear set is packaged in a miniature steamer trunk to enhance the traveling bear theme.

April Whitcomb Gustafson - The Roosevelt Bears

April Whitcomb Gustafson began collecting miniature bears at the age of six. Her bad case of myopia (nearsightedness) drew her to tiny things, as she says "the smaller, the better ... I was absolutely enchanted with miniature bears."

Even after her eyesight improved, her passion for small bears did not change. When she graduated from college and found full time work as a graphic artist, she began moonlighting and hand sculpting her very own miniature bears at home.

It didn't take long for April's miniature bears to catch on with collectors around the world, selling for between $100 and $1500 a piece. Unlike any other artist bear on the market today, April's original bears manage to look like stuffed bears, but are actually hand sculpted out of clay and covered with velvet "fur".

When she recently purchased one of Seymour Eaton's books at an antique show, she was drawn to the exquisitely detailed illustrations of The Roosevelt Bears. Now she has captured that detail in miniature sculpture and has a successful partnership with Schmid to manufacture and distribute these incredibly precise reproductions of the famous Roosevelt Bears. (See Section on Schmid, page 113.)

April Whitcomb Gustafson's latest venture with bears is sculpting the Roosevelt Bears which are reproduced by the Schmid Company.

The Boyds Collection Ltd. - The Bearstone Collection

The Boyds Collection (see page 105) has recently added a full line of figurines to its extensive offerings. This series is based on the already popular plush line and is called "Boyds Bears & Friends, The Bearstone Collection." All are done with a touch of humor and their unique personalities are enhanced with a hidden paw print which has been painted or embossed into each piece.

"Boyds Bears & Friends...The Bearstone Collection" is a series of bears, hares and tabby figurines based upon the best selling members of the plush line. *Courtesy The Boyds Collection, Ltd.*

114

Chapter Five

Advertising Bears

Bears have been an advertising symbol or logo since the 19th century. At first, true-to-life bears set the tone for definitive qualities such as strength and power. When teddy bears burst on to the scene in the early 20th century, their image could be marketed to impart feelings of sweetness, loyalty, reliability and soft affection.

Some of the most popular products using bears and teddy bears in their advertising campaigns include food and beverage products. Polar bears quickly bring up the thought of refreshing, cold delights and cuddly teddy bears are a sure fire visual image of sweet honey taste.

One of the first companies to take advantage of the bear in advertising was Pettijohn's Breakfast Food. Originally, the bear portraying the "Bear in Mind" trademark was a realistic looking bear, with a heavy fur coat. By 1902 the bear's look had softened and appeared more teddyish.

Seymour Eaton's Roosevelt Bears (see page 21) were a major catalyst in taking teddy bears to the printed page. Their story book concept published in the newspaper on a regular basis opened the door for the public to adjust to seeing a personified bear as a comfortable image.

Another early advertiser using the bear is Bear Brand Hosiery, an early manufacturer of silk and nylon stocking based in the midwest. At first, its logo was a grizzly bear. But, later on, this company too decided that a lovable teddy bear would be a much more suitable, and friendly image, for ladies hosiery products. The box featured a bear and several premiums came out in the early 20th century, one of which was a

"Teddy Bear Bread" calendar. Circa 1912. According to Terry and Doris Michaud (owners of the calendar), The Wagner Baking Company was located in Detroit, Michigan, and the granddaughter of the founder remembers seeing the huge plush bears displayed behind the lunch counter of the bakery. *Courtesy Terry and Doris Michaud.*

This huge bruin (40in [101cm]) was made for the Wagner Baking Company located in Detroit, Michigan to advertise their "Teddy Bear Bread." Made of apricot-colored mohair, glass eyes and stuffed with excelsior, this design has characteristics of American made bears, possibly Ideal (Circa 1908). Pictured with the bear is a 1907 Fleischmann Co., booklet: *The Teddy Bear's Baking School*, which depicted the Roosevelt Bears. *Courtesy Thelma Kimble.*

paper bear, complete with legs that moved. (Illustration at left.) The company also released a popular promotional item based on the Three Bears. These were three flat cloth bears, each holding a box of Bear Brand Hosiery and designed for cut-and-sew at home. This family was issued in the late 1920s.

Another gimmick incorporating teddy bears was put forward by the Wagner Baking Company, which marketed "Teddy Bear Bread" to bakers from the Midwest through the east. A few select shops (5-7, according to Terry and Doris Michaud's article "Teddy Bear Bread—A Tale That Bears Repeating" included in *Teddy Bear and friends®*, January/February 1986 issue) displayed a 40in (102cm) bear with apricot mohair, glass eyes and felt pads. It was stuffed with excelsior and could have been made by Ideal (c. 1908). This sort of teddy bear is one of the finest examples of early, commercially promotional bears that is still in existence today. (Page 115, bottom right.)

As advertisers recognized the value of teddy bears, it is surprising that it is still difficult to find teddy bear manufacturers utilizing teddy bears in their own advertising. Steiff did publish such cards including one showing a menagerie of Steiff stuffed animals boarding an arc. The

Left: More than 60 years ago (1928) the British company Bear Brand Hosiery Ltd. began as an importer of silk stockings from the Bear Brand Company of Chicago, Illinois. At first its logo was a grizzly bear but after a great deal of research; it was decided a lovable teddy bear would be a much more suitable image for ladies hosiery products. *Courtesy Susan Nicholson*

Below: Crayola Bears. 1986. 7in (19cm); (left to right) yellow, lavender, red and royal blue synthetic plush; plastic eyes (eye color matches plush); shaved snouts; black plastic noses; unjointed bodies; stationary heads. Each bear wears T-shirt with "Crayola" printed on front (T-shirt matches color of bear). Label reads: "1986 Graphics International Inc./Korea." Box of film shows example of size of bears. *Private collection.*

Right: Celestial Seasonings. "Sleepytime" Herb Tea Bear. 1986. 17in (43cm); dark brown acrylic plush; black felt eyelids; black plastic nose; unjointed arms and legs; stationary head; soft stuffing; wearing white nightshirt and red nightcap. Label sewn into body reads: "Trudy/Norwalk Conn./Cel. Seasoning/ Collectors Series." Tin of Celestial Seasonings "Sleepytime" Herb Tea stands next to bear. *Courtesy Pat Todd.*

Below: (Left to right) R. Dakin Crocker Spaniel Puppy. 1979. 11in (28cm); beige acrylic plush; wears medallion around neck (embossed on medallion "Crocker Spaniel." Label reads: "Made exclusively for Crocker National Bank 1979/R. Dakin Korea." Crocker Bank "Sunny" Bear. 1975. 14in (36cm); golden orange acrylic plush. Label reads: "Crocker Bank/Crocker National Bank 1975." Reverse of label reads: "Animal Fair Inc., (Shr. Foam)." Hershey's Bear. 5in (13cm); dark brown acrylic plush; white inset plush snout, inner ears and paw pads. Ideal Hershey's Bear. 1982. 13in (33cm); dark brown acrylic plush; white plush inner ears and paw pads; vinyl face; painted features. Label reads: "- Ideal Toy Corporation 1982/Newark N.J." *Courtesy Pat Todd.*

Morgan Importing Company (New York) also published a couple of cards advertising Steiff Bears in 1907.

Another well-known series of advertising postcards are the "Cracker Jack Bears" copyrighted in 1907 by B.E. Mooreland. These were large bruins colorfully used to advertise Cracker Jacks. A special promotion on the back of Cracker Jack boxes offered 16, free, beautiful postcards for mailing in ten sides of Cracker Jack boxes.

Collecting advertising art with bear graphics is yet another branch of the bear world that has opened up to arctophiles. A good reference book for any teddy bear advertising art background is Marty Crisp's *Teddy Bears in Advertising Art* (Hobby House Press, 1991).

Today, all we need to do is look around to see the bear's role in logo design and advertising. Sears carries a whole line of Winnie-The-Pooh clothing and related items; children's sugar flavored cereals have always incorporated bears. Whether its vitamins or T-shirts, Teddy Bears are every where you look!

(Front left) "Jordache" Bear. 1981. 19in (48cm); white acrylic plush; beige acrylic plush inset snout; glass eyes; unjointed body; wearing Jordache Levi's (an integral part of body) with red waistcoat and pink hat. Label reads: "1981 Toyland Div. of Caesarea Glenoit Ind Ltd./A License of Jordache Enterprises." (Center back) Russ Berrie & Co., Inc. "Toasten T. Bear The Kraft Marshmellow Fellow. 1981. 18in (46cm) seated; cinnamon colored acrylic plush; beige acrylic plush inset snout, inner ears and paw pads; plastic eyes; unjointed body. Wears tan felt vest with "I Love Kraft Marshmellow" patch. (Front right) Morris Airbear. 1993. 12in (31cm); dark gray curly acrylic plush; beige, curly plush inset snout, and paw pads; plastic eyes; unjointed body; wearing a white fur trimmed flight jacket, white scarf and goggles. Label reads: "'Morris Airbear' for Morris Air Corporation 1993. *Courtesy Pat Todd.*

Russ Berrie & Co., Inc. *Snuggle* Bears. 1986. (Left to right: 7in [18cm], 11in [28cm], 6in [15cm]) white curly acrylic plush (left and center) beige acrylic plush (right); plastic eyes; unjointed bodies; black nose; pink lined open mouth. Manufacturers label reads: "Snuggle/C 1986/Lever Brothers Company." Reverse of label: "Russ Berrie & Co., Inc. Oakland N.J.." *Snuggle* was used to advertise a fabric softener of the same name. The name of the bear varied throughout the world according to national variations in the name of the product. *Courtesy Pat Todd.*

(Left to right) Heide "Gummi Bear." 1988. 9in (23cm) seated; golden acrylic plush; pale beige inset snout; flat painted plastic eyes; red lined open mouth; unjointed body; stationary head; blue sun suit with "Heide" label stitched on front. Inside tag reads: "Hi, I'm the world renowned Gummi Bear. Imported to bring you lots of love and affection. My family dates back to 1869 when my ancestor Henry Heide, an immigrant from Germany started a candy company in America . . . ." Curity "Dy-Dee" Bear. 9in (23cm); seated position; medium brown acrylic plush; white inset snout; black pompom nose; red felt tongue; glass eyes; unjointed body; white diaper with the name "Curity" printed on front. Label reads: "Animal Fair/Eden Valley/MN." "Mrs. Fields" Bear. 8in (20cm); brown acrylic plush; plastic eyes; unjointed body. Wears red cap and knapsack. Label reads: "Made in Korea for Mrs. Fields Cookies." *Courtesy Pat Todd.*

(Left to right) "Teddy Grahams" Bear. 1990. 10in (25cm). Label reads: "Nabisco Brands." "Hungry Jack" Bear. 1991. 13in (33cm). Label reads: "Hungry Jack/The Pillsbury Company 1991." Hallmark "Ginger" Bear. 1987. Label reads: "Ginger Bear - 1987 Hallmark Co., Inc." *Courtesy Pat Todd.*

Numerous well-known companies appreciate the popularity of teddy bears and use their appealing image to promote their product. Pictured are promotional bears from McDonalds, New York Life, Avon, I Love Izod, Time Life Music, and Giorgio Beverly Hills. *Courtesy Pat Todd.*

Chapter Six
Smokey Bear

In 1994, Smokey Bear turns 50! He was conceived during World War II as a symbol against careless creation of fires which could be seen as targets by our enemies.

Receiving more public service air time and print space than any comparable entity, Smokey is without a doubt the most popular "spokesbear" ever created. A recent survey shows him only second to Santa Claus in recognizable icons among both children and adults.

A wartime poster demonstrated that an animal of the forest was the best messenger to promote the prevention of human-caused forest fires. That poster featured "Bambi" who was a natural subject since he, himself, had escaped a forest

SMOKEY SAYS—
Care will prevent 9 out of 10 forest fires!

On August 2, 1994, the Forest Service and War Advertising Council introduced a bear as the campaign symbol. This bear was to be black and brown and his expression intelligent, appealing, and slightly quizzical. To look his part, he would wear a traditional campaign hat. Albert Staehle, noted illustrator of animals worked with this description to paint the forest fire prevention bear. His art appeared in the 1945 campaign, and the advertising symbol was given the name Smokey Bear. This poster (by Staehle) showed Smokey Bear actively engaged in the business of forest fire prevention. Note Staehle's early portrait of Smokey Bear (1944) depicted him as rather austere. *Reprinted with permission of the USDA Forest Service. All Rights Reserved.*

fire in a popular Walt Disney® feature length animated cartoon. It was the forerunner to using a bear as a campaign symbol.

Since his birth during the era of radio and the big band sound in a Foote, Cone, Belding and Honing volunteer ad agency poster, Smokey's look has definitely changed. That first poster carried the caption: "Smokey says: Care will prevent 9 out of 10 forest fires" and showed Smokey actively dousing a campfire with water. A number of artists played a part in Smokey's evolution. His first portrait depicted him as rather austere. It took Rudy Wendelin, a Foote Cone contract artist, to personify and metamorphosize him into a warm, friendly bear. He removed his claws, replacing them with more gentle digits. Smokey's current image reflects the work of Chuck Kudenas for the 1965 campaign.

A living symbol of Smokey was rescued from a devastating forest fire in New Mexico in 1950. The badly burned cub was found clinging desperately to a tree. Firefighters christened him "Smokey." The event was publicized by national children's heroes such as Hopalong Cassidy and The Sons of the Pioneers. After his burns healed he moved to the National Zoo (Washington, D.C.) where he was the living symbol of the Cooperative Forest Fire Prevention Program (CFFP) until his death in 1976.

Capitan, New Mexico, where Smokey was discovered, still remains the site of a popular, free Smokey Museum, run by a long-time local resident, Dorothy Gray Gluck.

Even though most Smokey memorabilia is not date-marked, there are plenty of Smokey Bear items available for collecting.

The Ideal Toy Company made the First Smokey Bear in 1953. (Page 125.) The first plush Smokey had a vinyl head. Through the years the vinyl head became only a vinyl face and eventually evolved to a totally plush toy.

Other companies which have produced Smokey Bear plush toys include Knickerbocker, Dakin, and Three Bears, Inc., International Bonn Ton Toys, Inc. and J.J. Wind, Inc. are currently producing the toys. Sizes of Smokey Bears range from 3in (8cm) to 3ft (91cm).

It is not known how many different bears have been made in Smokey's image. In fact, new models are not made every year. One enhancement to plush Smokeys are certain pieces of equipment representing Smokey's symbol that add to their value. Maybe it's a shovel, a buckle, a hat and in some cases a badge.

Smokey appears both sitting and standing and even, on occasion, talking. One version would talk when a crank on its back was turned. Another had a pull string with several safety messages designed for children. These were made by both Knickerbocker and Ideal. Finding one that still works is rare!

The Junior Forest Ranger program began with commercial licensing in 1952. The first stuffed Smokey, produced by

Above: Various stages of Smokey Bear's life are pictured on the inside page of a 1955 Smokey Bear comic book published by Dell Publishing Co., New York. *Courtesy Richard C. Yokley.*

Right: After World War II, the War Advertising Council changed its name to the Advertising Council. In the years that followed, the focus of Smokey's campaign broadened to appeal to children as well as adults. In this 1955 poster Smokey Bear's image becomes more warm and friendly. *Reprinted with permission of the USDA Forest Service. All Rights Reserved.*

A significant chapter in Smokey's long history began early in 1950 when a burned cub survived a fire in the Lincoln National Forest near Capitan, New Mexico. Because this bear survived a terrible forest fire and won the love and imagination of the American public, many people mistakenly believe that this cub was the original Smokey Bear. After being nursed back to health (pictured here being treated by a veterinarian in Santa Fe), Smokey came to live at the National Zoo in Washington, D.C. as a living counterpart to the CFFP Program's fire prevention symbol. *Reprinted with permission of the USDA Forest Service. All Rights Reserved.*

(Front) Knickerbocker. Smokey Bear. Circa 1970. 13in (33cm); brown rayon plush; beige rayon plush paw pads; inset vinyl snout with open mouth; plastic eyes; unjointed body (seated position); blue jeans (an integral part of body); plastic Smokey buckle; plastic Smokey Ranger badge. (Back) Dakin. Smokey Bear. Circa 1977. 14in (36cm); brown acrylic plush head, paws and feet; inset beige acrylic plush snout with open mouth; plastic nose; unjointed (standing position); blue jeans (an integral part of body); plastic Smokey buckle; T-shirts (an integral part of body); plastic yellow hats. *Courtesy Richard C. Yokley.*

Ideal included an application form that a child could mail to the Forest Service, requesting enlistment in the Junior Forest Ranger program. The overwhelming response saw more than a half million youngsters enrolled during the first three years. By 1955, Smokey received so much mail that he was assigned his own zip code. Children still remain Smokey's most ardent supporters, many of them proudly owning a kit which contains letters from Smokey, a badge, a membership card and a wallet card.

In a cultural climate where 15 minutes of fame is the norm, Smokey has been kept alive by the public, the U.S. Forest Service, the Advertising Council and the National Association of State Foresters. In accordance with the Smokey Bear Act (1952), The Forest Service continues to license a wide variety of toys and other Smokey Bear items relating to fire prevention.

Smokey's forest fire prevention message is as important today as it was half a century ago. Children and adults still continue to heed the advice of the bear who tries hard to help us save our beautiful forests and wildlands from careless fire. Smokey's presence is a constant reminder to be safe indoors and out. All of us are never too old to: "Remember...Only YOU can prevent forest fires!"

If you want to learn more about Smokey Bear, his evolution is charted in *Guardian of the Forest, A History of the Smokey Bear Program* (Ellen Earnhardt Morrison).

Lincoln County rancher Don Brewer commissioned this commemorative painting from Smokey's personal painter, Rudolph Wendelin, then donated it to Friends of Smokey, a non-profit volunteer organization in Smokey's hometown of Capitan, New Mexico. *Courtesy Photograph by Michael J. Riska. Reprinted with permission of the U.S.D.A. Forest Service. All Rights Reserved.*

Jim Van Meter, a retired Fire Captain, is actively involved with fire prevention. He says that "adults seem to take Smokey for granted and often relegate him to the level of clown or entertainer. We need to look at Smokey through the eyes of a child and realize he is an educator. Millions of children have learned Smokey's rules of match safety. He got us through those early exploratory years without being burned by our curiosity, let alone starting a fire. Smokey means more to me than collectibles, profits and entertainment. He and his image become a powerful educational tool which affects the lives of children everywhere. After all 'children are our future.'" Jim is pictured with Smokey Bear at the National Celebration of Smokey Bear's 50th Anniversary in Washington D.C. (August 9, 1994). *Courtesy Captain Jim Van Meter.*

The second version of Ideal's Smokey Bear was produced in 1954. The bears are seated around a rare Smokey Bear barbecue and book *Letters to Smokey Bear* published by Grosset & Dunlap, New York (1966).

Ideal. Smokey Bear in original box. Circa 1960. 12in (31cm); unjointed body. *Private collection.*

Ideal Toy Company. "Smokey Bear", with original box. 1953. 18in (46cm); molded vinyl head; hands and feet stuffed with cotton; brown plush body; plastic eyes; painted features; incised on back of head "c. 1953/Smokey says/Prevent Forest Fires/Ideal Toy Company. "Original Smokey Bear design. Smokey came with separate hat, blue trousers, blue plastic shovel and silver badge which reads: "Smokey/Ranger/Prevent Forest Fires." and a silver belt buckle which reads: "Smokey." *Courtesy Barbara Baldwin.*

Knickerbocker. Smokey Bears. Circa 1973. Produced in sizes 12in (31cm), 14in (36cm), 16in (41cm), 24in (61cm), and 28in (71cm). Various shades of brown synthetic plush; with beige synthetic plush heart-shaped inset faces; black felt noses; red felt mouths; googlie-type plastic eyes. Note the resemblance in the face to Clifford K. Berryman's famous "Berryman Bear" cartoon character. Unjointed bodies (seated position) various shades of blue jeans (an integral part of body); plastic Smokey buckle; plastic Smokey badge. This design of bear was also produced with a talking mechanism encased in body. *Courtesy Richard C. Yokley.*

My grandchildren Frances Tipton (left) and Jenny Mullins (right) love my Smokey Bears. They never tire of hearing me tell the story of Smokey Bear. *Photograph by Larry McDaniel.*

Above: Dakin. Smokey Bears. (Left and center left) 1985. 13in (33cm) and 12in (31cm); brown acrylic plush; beige acrylic plush inset snout and around eyes; glass eyes; plastic noses; unjointed (seated position); blue jeans (an integral part of body); plastic Smokey buckle; yellow plastic hat. (Center right) 1980. 14in (36cm); (Right) 1983. 10in (25cm). Both center and center right are the same design: dark brown acrylic plush; light beige acrylic plush inset snout; plastic eyes; unjointed (standing position) blue jeans (an integral part of body) with plastic Smokey buckle, yellow plastic hat. *Courtesy Richard C. Yokley.*

Right: Three Bears Co. Smokey Bears. (Left to right) 1989. 12in (31cm), 1985. 30in (76cm), 1985. 6in (15cm), 1985. 15in (38cm). Cinnamon-colored acrylic plush; light beige acrylic plush inset snout and paw pads; brown fabric noses; plastic eyes; unjointed bodies (seated position); blue jeans (an integral part of body); gold-colored Smokey buckle; floppy beige fabric hat. *Courtesy Richard C. Yokley.*

Captain Richard C. Yokley, of the Bonita Fire Department in Southern California has been an avid Smokey Bear collector since 1977. Richard is pictured with some of his prized possessions. *Courtesy Richard C. Yokley.*

Good Bears of the World, a non-profit organization founded in 1973, is a shining example of teddy bear magic. Good Bears of the World (GBW) was conceived by James T. Ownby (photo below) to provide teddy bears to sick children and hospitalized adults, elderly people confined to nursing homes and abused children in shelters and foster homes. It was the first group to donate teddy bears to police departments in the early 1980s.

I am proud that my shows are one of the many arenas where funds and bears are contributed to this special club which boasts nearly 2000 members and 35 "dens" both here and abroad. Originally the association's headquarters were in Mr. Ownby's radio station in Hawaii, but the group relocated to Toledo, Ohio in 1991.

Peter Bull, (photo below) author of *Bear With Me* and *The Teddy Bear Book* greatly influenced the founder of GBW. After reading about one man's (Russell McClean) efforts to utilize teddy bears to dispel the negative emotions hospitalize children so often endure, Ownby said "It is patently obvious that this project should be taken up on a worldwide basis." And so it was.

One of GBW's greatest supporters is Bill Boyd, who also was greatly influenced by Peter Bull. He met Jim Ownby in 1979 and since that time he has not missed a copy of the organization's quarterly publication, *Bear Tracks*, and has furthered the cause of GBW by leaps and bounds.

Jim Ownby died in 1986. Peggy Maxwell and Leona Jona struggled to keep the organization alive from Honolulu. The task was not easy as there were no funds and the strong leadership of Jim, who traveled worldwide, was not there to maintain the momentum he had achieved. In 1989 Peggy visited Bill Boyd in his home and during that time, Bill offered to do a fund raiser for GBW and become its Goodwill Ambassador (see page 130, top). In 1990, he produced the first Teddy Bear Jubilee in Kansas City which raised $6700 to help keep the organization afloat. Every year since, Bill has repeated the project. In 1993 the event brought in $8000.

The 25th Anniversary of GBW is in 1994. There is a special bear only available during the anniversary year. The bear will be limited to an edition of 5000 and is made by Muffin Enterprises. Appropriately named Silver, the gray plush bear will be issued with a special certificate, a hang tag with the history of Good Bears of the World, and a black neck ribbon imprinted with the GBW logo. (See page 130, top.)

Coinciding with the 25th anniversary of GBW was the 50th birthday of Smokey Bear. To commemorate this milestone year, the United States Department of Agriculture Forestry Service commissioned internationally renowned teddy bear artist Robert Raikes to create a limited edition of only 15 hand-made (original) "Smokey Bears." These bears were used by the Forest Services throughout this anniversary year to honor Smokey Bear and everyone of them will be donated to a charity for fund raising purposes. Each Smokey Bear stands 42in (106cm); has an authentic Smokey Bear brass belt buckle, denim pants, campaign hat and hand-carved wooden face and felt paw pads. The bears are fully jointed. Ever a loyal supporter of Good Bears of the World, Robert Raikes has donated two of these rare bears for fund raising work of gifting teddy bears to traumatized children and the forgotten elderly. The only way to get one of these bears was to win a raffle. One GBW Smokey was raffled at the Toy Store's Tribute to Teddies XIII in Toledo, Ohio and the other through my show in San Diego (Linda's Teddy Bear, Doll and Antique Toy Show and Sale).

After 25 years, GBW is still vigorous and growing! This caring group is supported entirely by membership and donations and will continue to gift teddies to traumatized children and the forgotten elderly for a long time to come.

For GBW Club information write to: Good Bears of the World, Box 13097, Toledo, OH 43613.

Two men who have contributed so much to the world of teddy bears: (Left) the late Jim T. Ownby founder of Good Bears of the World. (Right) the late Peter Bull. Peter was responsible for bringing the teddy bear collectors of the world together through his first book, *The Teddy Bear Book* (1969, Random House).

Bill Boyd is Goodwill Ambassador and second Vice-President of Good Bears of the World. Bill attends many events promoting Good Bears of the World (G.B.W.). Bill was presented "G.B.W.'s Fund Raising Wizard" trophy by G.B.W. in 1993. Pictured with Bill are G.B.W. bears including their silver plush 25th Anniversary bear (limited edition of 5,000 or less).

Above: G.B.W. members Marilyn and Lee Lewis enjoy donating their time representing G.B.W. at teddy bear events. At my teddy bear shows in San Diego participating artists, collectors and I donate bears for the raf fle to benefit G.B.W. 1994 was the 25th Anniversary of G.B.W.

Left: Ever a loyal supporter of Good Bears of the World (G.B.W.) Robert Raikes has donated two of his 15 rare Smokey Bears to G.B.W . for raising funds to carry on the work of gifting teddy bears to traumatized children and the for gotten elderly. Each Smokey Bear stands 42in (106cm); has hand-carved wooden face, feet and paw pads and an authentic Smokey Bear brass belt buckle, denim pants, and campaign hat. The bears are fully jointed.

Chapter Eight

Teddy Bear Restoration

Of great interest to collectors of old and antique teddy bears is that of caring for and restoring these most prized and valuable possessions.

In addition to her fame as an accomplished teddy bear artist (P.J. Bears), Patricia Johnson has also gained national recognition as the "Teddy Bear Doctor." This talented and caring lady, called Patsy by her friends, brings happiness to so many people with her painstaking methods of restoring, resurrecting and even reincarnating well-loved teddy bears. Without Patsy, these precious little characters, that have spent their lives sharing love and hugs, may have otherwise been tossed away and lost forever. Patsy appears at numerous conventions, shows and private seminars throughout America. She is continuously asked by collectors to write a book on this very important subject.

I was delighted when Patsy agreed to my request for her to write an in-depth chapter in this book and share with you her vast knowledge of teddy bear restoration.

Patricia Johnson's Teddy Bear Restoration Methods

If you have a dear old bear, one you grew up with, or one your relatives have just found...what should you do with it? How should you care for it?

If you are the owner of a "new" old bear, you probably are so happy just to have found him that you don't want him changed a bit. You like him looking old with "holey" pads that leak stuffing or limbs that no longer hold their shape. Maybe you have already spent more on him that you should have and don't want to invest any more money. Perhaps these suggestions will help you to keep your investment in the same condition you obtained him in. If a bear is carefully cleaned and repaired or restored, it certainly adds value.

In restoring bears there is no one way to do anything. Each bear has somewhat different problems. Be creative in thinking through each problem and what resources you have available or can obtain to best solve the problem.

I have used all of these methods described. However, I have worked with fabrics all my life and have had many years of designing experience. If you do not feel comfortable handling your bear, please find a professional to repair it. Ask to see some of their work or get references.

If you have sensitive hands, it is advisable to wear gloves of some kind when removing stuffing or when doing any repair on a bear. If you have respiration problems, wear a mask. Old bears can be very dirty and dusty.

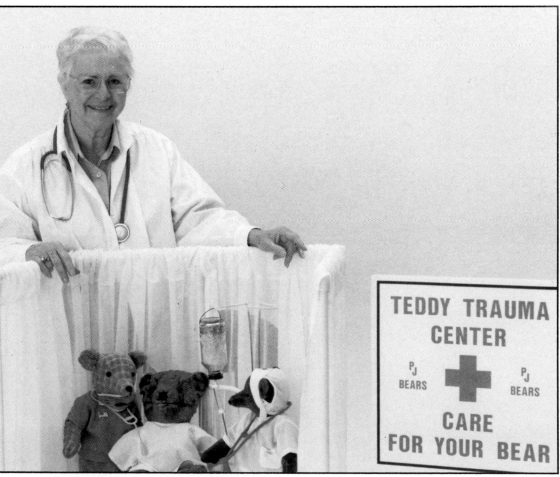

Patricia's warm smile makes her new clients feel at ease when they bring their beloved sick teddy bears for her to repair at her "Teddy Trauma Center." Courtesy Patricia Johnson. *Photograph by Harvey Henningsen.*

Cleaning

Cleaning your bear will be one of the most effective ways of improving his appearance. Type of bear and condition determine what product to use in cleaning. For a mohair, wool, or lightly soiled bear, the product to use is a mild baby clothes soap powder. Fill a blender half way with warm water, then add about two tablespoons of soap. Run the blender until there is a good "head" of suds. Using just the suds and a damp wash cloth, rub gently or pat the suds on a small area. Work them into the nap. Some of the suds will go into the fabric backing cleaning it as well. Work a small area at a time, starting with the head. Use another damp cloth to rinse off the suds and dirt. Sometimes it is necessary to use three or four wash cloths and keep rinsing them in clear water. Do not get your bear wet below the fabric. The surface should just be damp at this point. If there are some very dirty spots, you can return to them later. (See top photo below.)

Continue in this manner until you have covered the entire surface of your bear. You may then use a weak solution of fabric softener and water. Use a teaspoon of softener to three cups of water. Go over the entire bear lightly with more clean washcloths. Rinse the wash cloth often in the softener solution, again being careful not to get the bear wet below the fabric. At this point, use a small finger wire brush or a bristle brush and very carefully pull or coax the hairs to stand up. On a very large bear, a small curry comb works well. (See bottom photo below.)

Note: be very careful with old brittle bears not to snag or tear the backing material.

Your bear will begin to look great! Let him dry on a sweater dryer or a place where air can circulate.

Never place your bear in the sun to dry as sun can change his color. Do not use a hair dryer because heat sets stains. Do not handle your bear at this point or you will pack the nap down. When dry, check for spots. If there are some you can't live with, repeat the whole process, or just clean the spots with a good upholstery cleaner. Follow the directions on the cleaner including testing for color fastness. Rinse as you did before and dry again.

If the mohair or wool bear is very soiled, begin with the upholstery cleaner, as it is easier on the fabric. Always rinse away all the cleaner so as not to leave cleaning residue. Brush as before and let dry.

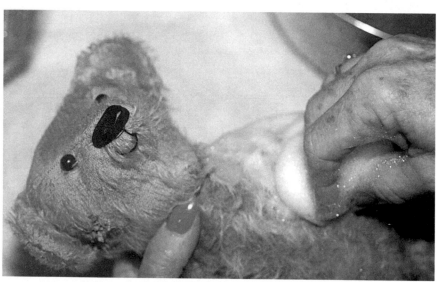

Cleaning your bear is one of the most effective ways of improving his appearance. *Courtesy Patricia Johnson.*

Tools for brushing your bear. *Courtesy Patricia Johnson.*

If you have a multicolored rayon, Dacron or other synthetic fabric bear (such as a Panda) and it is heavily soiled, take it completely apart, wash the colors separately, fluff dry in the drier and resew. There is risk involved, but this is the only way I know to get white synthetic bears white again.

Repairing Holes and Seams

During the bathing process you may have noticed some thread breaks in the seams or small holes in the fabric backing of the bear. Use tapestry wool from a needlepoint shop to mend them. Holes in the fabric backing can be rewoven. Run your needle into the hole and bring it out about a 1/2in (1cm) into the fabric, working back and forth in one direction. When going in the other direction, pick up every other thread so that you are actually weaving a new piece of fabric from your thread. Keep the thread under the fabric so that it does not show. If you can see the thread as you sew, it will show when you are finished. Do not try to weave perfectly, as that is more obvious than some uneven stitching.

Get professional help if the fabric is very old and brittle. The older and more brittle the fabric, the larger the area you must use so that you have more bear fabric to hold your stitches. Do not pull the stitches tight. That strains the fabric.

The next most frequently used stitch to work on bears is the "ladder" stitch. Pick up a few threads on one side to be stitched and then go directly across the seam and pick up a few threads on the other side. Always work the point of your needle in the same direction. This stitch closes seams, sews up the back (or opening) of the bear after restuffing. It also attaches or reattaches ears. (page 133, bottom right). If the fabric is brittle, use deep stitches into the stuffing. Again, keep your stitching loose.

Top: Before restoration. *Courtesy Patricia Johnson.*

Middle: After Patsy (as Patricia is called by her friends) has restored the bear in the illustration above. *Courtesy Patricia Johnson.*

Bottom: Other than reweaving, the "ladder" stitch is the most frequently used stitch to work on bears. To make this stitch pick up a few threads on one side to be stitched and then go directly across the seam and pick up a few threads on the other side, always working the point of your needle in the same direction. The ladder stitch is used to close seams, sew up the back (or opening) of the bear after restuffing and to attach or reattach ears. *Courtesy Patricia Johnson.*

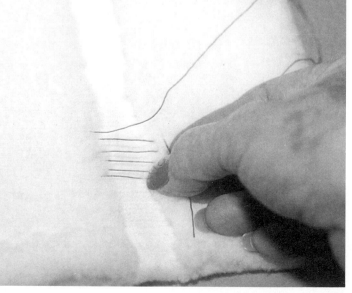

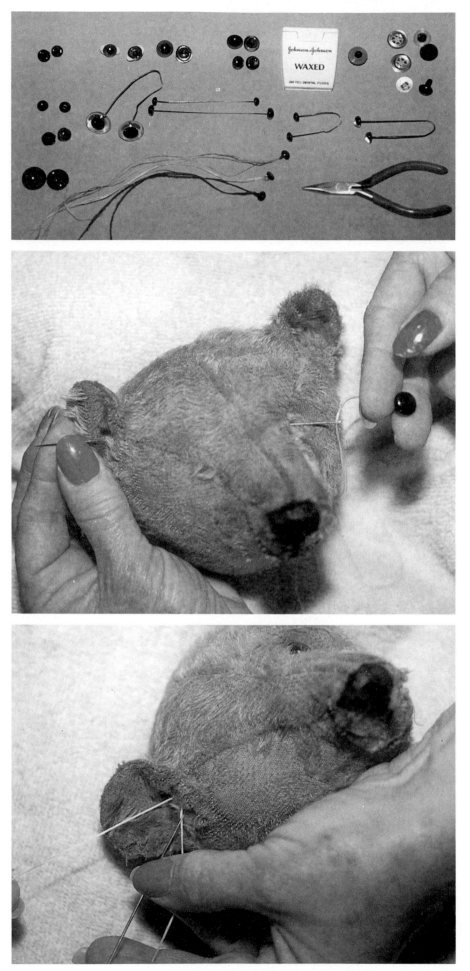

Replacing Eyes

Very loved bears frequently lose their eyes. Older bears have eyes that are either shoe buttons or glass eyes on metal posts. Glass eyes come two ways: with a wire loop in back or with a short piece of wire with eyes at each end. (See top left photo.) The latter style necessitates cutting the wire about 1in (3cm) from each eye. Make a loop with small pliers. Secure the end of the wire so that it will not tear the fabric behind the eye when in place.

Waxed dental floss, heavy waxed thread, or upholstery thread all can be used to attach the eye to the bear. Cut a piece about 40in (10cm) long, fold it in half, fold it again, making a loop of four strings. Place the center through the loop of the eye wire. Draw the ends of floss or thread through the loop and pull tightly. With small pliers flatten the wire loop so that it will fit into the small hole where the eye will go.

Divide the strands of floss or thread in half, placing two strands through the eye of a 6in (15cm) doll needle. Place the point of the needle in the exact spot where the original eye was. Push the needle behind the nose and out in the place where the opposite ear has been attached. Pull the floss through and off the needle. Thread the remaining two threads of floss through the needle, enter the eye at the exact spot as you did before so that when you tie a knot you will have some thread to secure it. Tie a knot making it as inconspicuous as possible. Then thread two strands of floss or thread onto the needle and bring it out in the back of the head, skip several threads, run it back into the fabric and bring it out another place and clip it close to the fabric. Repeat the process with the other two threads. By doing this you have buried the floss or thread in the head and secured the knots. (See middle and bottom photos.)

Top: A representation of eyes used on old and new bears. Patsy uses long nose pliers when attaching some of the eyes. *Courtesy Patricia Johnson.*

Middle: Patsy's method for attaching eyes. Insert long needle into eye space, come out at ear. Please refer to photo below for method of securing eye. *Courtesy Patricia Johnson.*

Bottom: Securing eye after the first step. (Above photo.) Tie threads close to ear so it does not show. *Courtesy Patricia Johnson.*

Modern bears have plastic safety eyes with a flat metal or plastic disk that snaps on the post of the eye with the fabric of the bear between the eye and the disk. Once the safety disk is in place it is difficult to remove the eye. Sometimes the post breaks and a new safety eye is needed to replace it.

To repair this type of eye, open the seam above the eye and remove any part of the old eye that may remain. If the fabric is weak or brittle, or there is a hole, put a small piece of lightweight strong fabric behind the eye and tack it in place with invisible stitches. If necessary sew up the hole so that the eye will not fall into the bear's head. Insert the replacement eye in the original piece. Through the opening of the seam insert the safety disk and snap it onto the post behind the eye. Restuff the area and use the ladder stitch to sew the original seam together.

Restoring or Replacing Paw Pads

The most common problem with bears is mending or replacing paw pads. The original fabric is usually wool felt. If you don't have access to 100% wool felt, find an old wool felt hat at a used clothing store. Some teddy bear suppliers have good wool felt dyed in the color of paw pads. Dip these new pieces into either tea or coffee to make them look more used. If you need to dye the felt to match, see the section on dyeing fabrics (top right photo.)

To make a pattern for the new paw pads, place the felt or fabric over the old pad. To mark the shape of the pad, pin with glass headed pins. Very few bear's foot and hand pads are exactly the same size. If you are doing both, try to make your pattern from the largest pad and trim the other to fit. Carefully cut around the pin line, taking care not to cut into the bear itself. (I suggest using applique scissors to protect the bear fabric). Cut out this piece. Remove the pins as you cut. Leave 1/8in (.31cm) seam allowance. (See page 136, top left.) Make foot pads in the same way. **Caution:** Do not use the craft felt sold today in most fabric stores.

Turning under the seam allowance, pin the pad in place on the foot and then sew it on with a very small invisible stitch. Be very gentle. If the fabric is brittle, be more careful to protect the fabric than about hiding stitches. Do not remove any original felt or fabric from the bear.

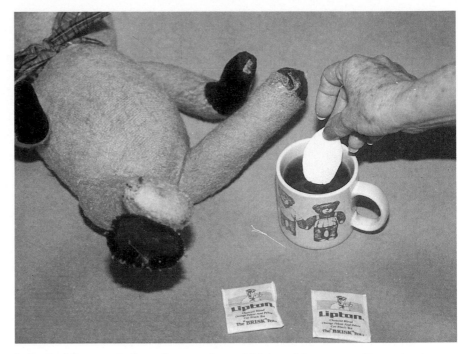

Aging the felt paw pads. Patsy dips new pieces of felt into either tea or coffee to give them an older look and one that would appear more original to the bear. *Courtesy Patsy Johnson.*

Making a pattern for a new foot pad. Place the felt or fabric over the old pad, pinning with glass headed pins. This marks the shape of the pad. Very few bear's foot and hand pads are exactly the same size. If you are doing both, try to make your pattern from the largest pad and trim the other to fit. Carefully cut around the pin line taking care not to cut into the bear itself. (Applique scissors with the large bottom blade are handy to protect the bear fabric). Cut out this piece removing the pins as you cut. Leave a 1/8in (.31cm) seam allowance. The same method is used for the paw (hand) pads. *Courtesy Patricia Johnson.*

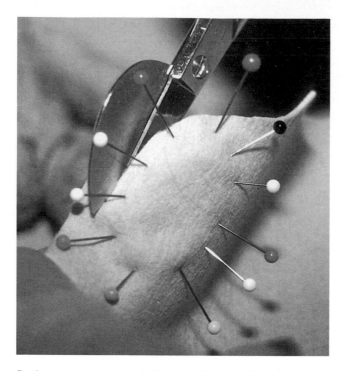

Cutting out a new paw pad. *Courtesy Patricia Johnson.*

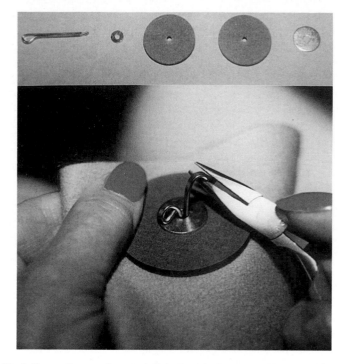

(Top) Cotter pins, washers and disks for jointing bears. (Bottom) Bending cotter pin to tighten joint. *Courtesy Patricia Johnson.*

Underlining Paw Pads

If there is felt left on the paw pads, leave it there and place matching felt under the original. Tack it in with small stitches.

Occasionally, some of the stuffing has been lost so that you must replace it. Try to replace it with what was there originally. (If it was excelsior, see note on excelsior.) Some bears have cardboard pads under their felt pads. If so, you will need to replace lost or damaged pads, slightly smaller than the paw pad. The cardboard can be covered with either felt or Ultrasuede.

Restuffing

Unless there is a major problem with the stuffing, it is generally better not to restuff a bear. However, some of the early American character or carnival bears have been stuffed with ground rags or shredded foam rubber. The latter deteriorates and becomes flat and sticky. Over the years, ground rags can pick up moisture creating an odor. Also, it easily packs down and becomes lumpy. If that is the case, the stuffing should be removed and discarded. Bears constructed of rayon, Dralon or synthetic plush may be hand washed. Restuff the bear with good polyester fiberfill.

Mohair bears sometimes get out of shape because the excelsior (wood shavings) breaks down, compacts or disintegrates. When this happens, open a seam and add a small amount of the original material, being careful not to damage the covering material. Old bears do not need to be stuffed firmly as this adds stress on fabric and takes away the soft and lovable appearance.

Unless you are experienced in restoration, please do not do this for any rare mohair bear. Have someone with experience take over!

Tightening Joints

If the arm, leg or head hangs loose or is wobbly, it can increase the wear and tear on the bear. When an arm, leg, or head has come off of a jointed bear, it means the disk (usually cardboard) has been damaged, or that the metal fastener (usually a nail) is broken. The center back or front seam that has been sewn by hand must be opened. This is usually sewn with very course thread or string. Save this string and put it inside the bear if you cannot reuse it. Remove and save the stuffing around the joint to be repaired as you will to reuse it when you have made the repair.

Next, open the seam on the limb or head sufficiently to allow access to the joint. Remove the stuffing around the disk and repair the joint. You may need to use a cotter pin to replace the nail. To do this, place the washer (or replace it with a metal washer if it is broken, bent or rusty) over the ends of the cotter pin. If the original disk is still stable and flat, use it. If not, replace it. The cotter pin with the washer and disk is inserted into the limb. The ends of the cotter pin exit through the original hold of the limb into the body that corresponds with that joint.

On the inside of the body, place another disk (if possible, original) and then a metal washer. The cotter pin is then opened, bent into a curl so that it holds the washer and disk in place (top right photo). It is not necessary to make this joint so tight that it is difficult to move. When finished, it should move easily. Replace the stuffing in the limb and sew it together with the ladder stitch. If the bear's fabric is very worn, or the cotter pin hole is too large, place a piece of strong material on the inside of the fabric and stitch with invisible stitches to reinforce it.

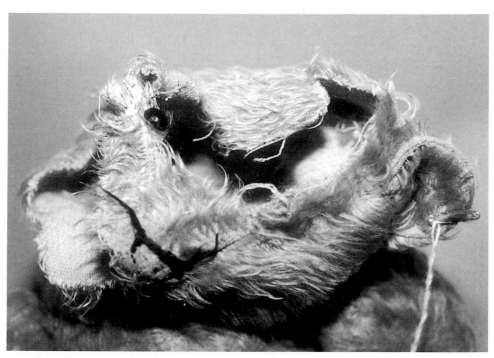

Right: This poor early 1900s teddy had experienced tremendous damage to his head. However, after Patsy's "tender loving care" the bear was restored to his natural beauty (photo below). *Courtesy Patricia Johnson.*

Below: This bear is an excellent example of the outstanding workmanship of Patsy Johnson's restoration abilities. It is hard to believe he is the same bear as the devastating picture of him in the photo at right. *Courtesy Patricia Johnson.*

A variety of growlers and squeakers Patsy has found in the teddy bears she has restored over the years. Courtesy Patricia Johnson.

When bear joints are intact, but so loose they cannot hold their heads up, the cardboard disk may have lost its stiffness. The seam above the joint will have to be opened up. The process is the same as before, but many times the old cardboard disk can just be reversed. The cotter pin when tightened will force the bowed disk back into shape so that the joint is more stable. Or it may simply need a little more stuffing added to the limb or body under the head.

Try to do as little as possible so that the bear remains in as close to original condition as possible. Any time you open a bear you make a note of what was done and when it was done, so that in the future the history of the bear will be more accurate.

Ear Restoration

If the ears are off or loose, they can be attached with the ladder stitch and matching thread. Generally it is not hard to tell where the ear was because there is a line or wear mark. Be careful that you sew the ear in the right place, as it definitely changes the bear's expression to have the ears moved. He will look angry if you put them further back than they were. Generally the edges of the ears get the dirtiest and most worn so they need the most cleaning and mending. (See page 133, top and middle.) If an ear is missing, replace it. (See the section on Replacing Missing or Torn Fabric.)

Restore Nose, Mouth or Claws

Use thread that matches the original. Pearl cotton is generally used. You may want to dip it in pure bleach to take off the sheen. Rinse and dry before using. Restitch in original place. If you are unclear of the original appearance, research for a picture of your bear to guide you.

Replacing Missing or Torn Fabric

Dogs, cats and jealous lovers can be very hard on teddies. Teeth holes in bear "hide" can be "grafted." To do this, take the fabric from some less noticeable part of the bear, between the neck joint, the back or the bear's bottom and use it to replace the torn or missing fabric. Then find the same type of fabric to replace this fabric. These bears restore nicely, as a rule, but can be very time consuming and expensive.

On new bears that have met up with a playful puppy, it is sometimes possible to reweave the backing material and replace the plush with Persian wool from the needlepoint shop. This is easier than dyeing fabric to match. Use the embroidery turkey stitch to attached the yarn. Trim the yarn even with the nap and if you are lucky, you will have a good match. If the backing of the bear is fragile and does not hold together, you may be able to match it with Persian yarn. Use a weaving technique. Reinforce the backing material.

Restoring Growlers and Squeakers

My experience tells me that a non-functioning growler or squeaker is just as well left alone. However, they can sometimes be repaired. Most of them operate on the principle of a bellows forcing air through a restriction in a tube causing the sound. When the restrictor or reed is missing, or the covering of the bellows has holes, air can no longer be forced through the tube. Kidskin, duct tape or even bellows cloth from a piano company can sometimes be applied onto the outside of the growler or squeaker to contain the air. (See photo above.) Be very careful when using glue in or on an old bear as it can damage the surface of the bear.

Resurrection

When bears have lost ears or limbs and need new ones, there is a real challenge. You need to find the same type of fibers with the same number of fibers per square inch and same length of plush. Try to get the backing material as close as possible to the original. Teddy bear supply houses have a good supply of different plush fabrics which makes it less difficult to find the correct fabric. The color is not as important because it usually has been dyed to match anyway. It should be understood that it is almost impossible to get a perfect color match as each dye process will give a slightly different color and different fabrics will reflect light differently.

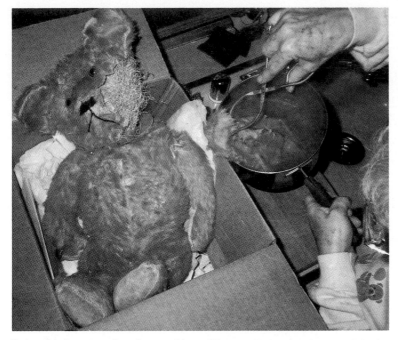

Dying fabric to match a damaged bear. Please refer to the photo at right for picture of bear after restoration. *Courtesy Patricia Johnson.*

The bear (in the photo at left) after Patsy dyed the mohair and carefully attached it to the damaged area. Patsy's restoration is truly a work of art! *Courtesy Patricia Johnson.*

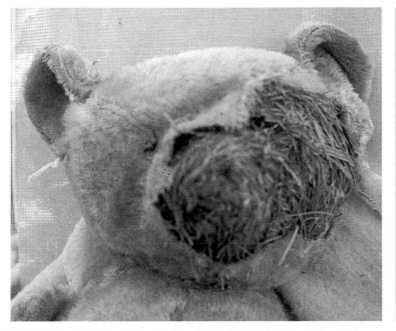

To "reincarnate" a bear is a very drastic measure and of course used only on bears that have no hope for restoring. It does take quite a lot of experience to fill in those missing pieces. Please refer to the photo at right to see the magnificent restoration Patsy performed on this poor "faceless" bear. *Courtesy Patricia Johnson.*

Restored "faceless" bear. Please refer to the photo at left to see how badly this bear was damaged before Patsy's restoration. *Courtesy Patricia Johnson.*

Patience is also required in making an acceptable match. (See top left and right photos.) Once I dipped a piece of fabric and let it dry 256 times before it was alright.

Use ordinary fabric dye and choose colors to blend to match the color of the bear. This may take some educated guess work. The material should be wet. Keep the dye bath and the material about the same temperature. Dip the material into the dye with tongs. Take it out after a few seconds and rinse it in water. Adjust the dye color if required. The fabric is always a different color when dried; usually lighter. (This is why you need to dry the fabric between dippings.) If the color is too dark, start all over. (Bleaching may also obtain the proper match.)

To "age" a new fabric, tie it in knots, wrap it with string, smudge it, and dip it into a liquid like tea or coffee.

In replacing a missing ear, take the existing ear off the bear. Then, turn it inside out and remove the stitching, leaving two pieces. Use these pieces as patterns to cut two new pieces to match. Right side together, stitch the old piece with a new one. Turn to the right side and sew the two ears onto the bear with the old fabric to the front of the bear, new fabric to the back. Stitch along the original seam line.

Reincarnation

Bears that are nearly without hope of salvation do not need to be thrown out. I try to take them apart, underline them with similar material and carefully put them back together again. Sometimes it takes experience to fill in the missing pieces. (See page 139, bottom left and right photos.) The edge of the original fabric is tacked or woven onto underlining. This also takes patience. Leave this to a professional!

SPECIAL NOTES:

Excelsior: When using new excelsior, it is wise to bake it for several hours at 200 ° F to ensure the drying sap which could stain or spot your bear. Dampen the excelsior to soften it before use.

Insect Damage: To prevent moth or other insect damage to bears, make small bags or envelopes of lace and fill them with cedar chips from the pet store. Seal or tie the bags and place them around the bears. Make cushions for the bear to sit on using the same method. Bay leaves are also good for use as an insect repellent. If your bear comes to me with suspicious holes that appear to be made by insects, he will spend some time in our deep freezer to kill any insects and eggs.

Pat Johnson, PJ Bears
Teddy Trauma Center
2121 Contra Costa Avenue
Santa Rosa, CA 95405
(707) 578-8809

SOURCES FOR FABRIC AND SUPPLIES

Edinburgh Imports
P.O. Box 772
Woodland Hills, CA 91365-0722
In California Call (818) 591-3800
Call outside of California (800) EDINBERG

Intercal
P.O. Box 11337
Costa Mesa, CA 92627
(714) 646-4025

Bear Street
415 West Foothill Blvd.
Claremont, CA 91711
(714) 625-2995

Bear Clawset
27 Palermo Walk
Long Beach, CA 90803
(213) 434-8077

Patsy Johnson matches the color of Persian yarn to the bear at her local needle point shop. *Courtesy Patricia Johnson.*

Index

Other Distinguished Reference Books by the Author

Linda Mullins is regarded as the premier Teddy Bear Show promoter in America. She is a leading authority in teddy bear collecting.

Tribute to Teddy Bear Artists

What is teddy bear art? Who are teddy bear artists? Discover the myriad of answers through the personal accounts of 130 popular teddy bear artists from around the world. These artists are members of an elite fraternity of creative people who are able to express unique feelings with unprecedented freshness and vitality. They share their woes and joys in personal accounts of their very first bear creations as well as sharing bear making tips ranging from easy nose designing to correct fur stitching. Learn these tricks of the trade and ways to market you own bear creations from their expertise! 160 pages. 300 photos. 8½" x 11". HB. Item #4742. $29.95

4th Teddy Bear & friends® Price Guide

Latest values on bears, rabbits, cats and dogs as well as a wealth of other animals are featured! This book shows and values what is being collected today! Such important collectibles as Muffy, antique, collectible, manufacturer and artist are featured as well as a large section devoted to such popular companies as Steiff, North American Bear, Gund and limited editions from Steiff Museum Collection. Charts as well as 358 stunning photographs capturing the character of bears and their friends. 176 pages. 118 color photos. 6" x 9". PB. Item #H4438. $12.95

Teddy Bears Past & Present, Volume I

Regarded as THE COLLECTOR'S IDENTIFICATION GUIDE, this volume contains a wealth of critical background information on the history of leading bear manufacturers and over 600 photographs, 80 in color, of the bears they produced. *Teddy Bears Past & Present* makes it easy to determine the price of your favorite bears because of its visual and chronological order. Best presentation about the distinguishing characteristics of bears, labels and tags. 304 pages. 8½" x 11". HB. Item #3120. $29.95

Teddy Bears Past & Present, Volume II

As the companion to Volume I, *Teddy Bears Past & Present, II* provides more in depth research into the gems of the history of the teddy bear. This research includes such diverse topics as today's bruin collecting and manufacturing in Germany, America, Britain, Australia, Japan and France as well as biographies of elite teddy bear artists and a wealth of photographs of their bears. Over 500 photos, 153 in stunning full-color. 304 pages. 8½" x 11". HB. Item #H4330. $25.00

The Raikes Bear & Doll Story (Revised Edition)

Revised values with many new photos. Robert Raikes fans have something new to cheer about! An exquisite photograph album and very readable story of how Raikes' phenomenal bears came to be and their evolution into one of the hottest bear collectibles ever. Includes fascinating photos of the early carvings through the bears and dolls produced in 1993 as well as some exquisite one-of-a-kind pieces. 120 pages. 250 photographs, 167 in color! 8½" x 11". HB. Item #H4654. $22.95